SACRED ECHOES

By:

Dawna Lindsey

SACRED ECHOES Copyright © Dawna Lindsey, 2024

Although the author and publisher have made every effort to ensure the accuracy and completeness of the information contained in this book, we assume no responsibility for errors, inaccuracies, omissions, or any inconsistencies herein. Any slights on people, places, or organizations are unintentional.

Dedication

To all those who have walked beside me on this journey of faith, whose wisdom, love, and presence have echoed the sacred in my life. Thank you for your inspiration and support.

Lord,

Four years ago, I wrote the vision. I was uncertain about how, or even if, You would bring it to fruition. Still, I placed my trust in Your perfect plan, holding fast to the belief that if I truly delighted in You, You would grant me the desires of my heart. How deeply personal You are! Just when I think I've come to understand Your nature, You surpass my every expectation. Repeatedly, You craft unique moments that allow me to connect with You on a multitude of levels. I cherish these instances and vow never to take them for granted, striving always to be rooted in gratitude. My motives extend beyond mere material gain or acclaim; I aim to shine Your glory. My life stands as a testament to the transformative power of Your mercy. With every divine encounter, You realign the orientation of my heart. May each instant serve as a tribute and every deed as a consecration. I vividly remember those solitary, dark nights when Your comforting presence was my only hope, the moments of tears, sorrow, and grief, but also the unparalleled joy and warmth of Your closeness. Even during the phases, I lost my way, only to return, it has always been for You. I lay it all at Your feet, surrendering every part of me.

Amen.

TABLE OF CONTENT

Dawna Lindsey

ECHOES OF FAITH

Let them praise the name of the Lord: for His name alone is excellent; His glory is above the earth and heaven" Psalms 148:13. In Old Testament times, a name was merely an identification marker. A name also encapsulates one's identity. Often, significant meanings were attached to names, serving explanatory and reflective purposes. In the Book of Daniel, Chapter 1, verse 17, it says, "As for these four youths, God gave them learning and skill in all literature and wisdom, and Daniel had understanding in all visions and dreams." This reflects the positive connotation of the name Daniel, emphasizing wisdom and understanding.

God's self-revelation in Scripture often comes through the names He adopts. A study of these divine epithets illuminates various aspects of God's character and deepens our understanding of His very essence. The significant meanings behind these names unfurl the core personality and inherent nature of the Almighty.

Who is God? To me, the Bible has always been more than mere ink on paper. It pulses with life, every word echoing the timeless presence of God amidst His people. Immersing myself in its passages, I've never felt like a mere spectator. Instead, I find myself actively woven into its sacred drapery. The struggles, aspirations, and dreams of biblical figures reflect my own, showcasing the universality of the human experience in the presence of the Divine.

In the vast expanse of human existence and our search for meaning, this question reverberates across the ages. Do you perceive Him as the Most High God, the All-Sufficient One, the Master, the Lord of Peace, or perhaps as the Lord who Provides? Perhaps you feel a more intimate connection, addressing Him as 'Father.' Amidst our varied interpretations and beliefs, it is paramount that we never diminish God to a mere abstract entity or a distant force merely receiving our prayers. He is Jehovah Raah, our ever-guiding Shepherd.

For just as God intimately knows each of us by name, so too should we strive to know Him by His name genuinely. Culminating in a harmonious symphony, God's name has echoed throughout scripture from the beginning to the end. Each divine appellation serves as a note, revealing facets of His character and weaving a majestic narrative that spans the entirety of the biblical story. In the names, from the psalms exalting the excellence of the Lord's name to the meanings attached to individuals like Daniel, we find a continuous melody that resonates with wisdom, understanding, and the timeless essence of the Almighty. Through the rich array of names, God's self-revelation unfolds, creating a symphony that transcends time and invites us to explore the depths of His infinite nature.

An echo, by definition, occurs when a sound encounters a hard surface and is reflected in the direction from which it came. But like the moments of revelation in our lives, echoes are not constant. They do not respond to every sound that graces our ears; rather, they select their moments carefully, waiting for the right resonance, the perfect alignment of circumstances and emotions. In the same way, the sacred echoes in our lives do not manifest in response to every experience. They are elusive, enigmatic, and deeply personal. They emerge when the conditions are right, when the heart is open, and when the soul is receptive to their message.

In the stillness of our lives, as the world buzzes with its endless cacophony, a hallowed echo persists. It is a divine whisper, cutting through the chaos, drawing us nearer to God's heart. This voice, ageless and powerful, winds its way from the annals of ancient scriptures, bridges epochs, and speaks directly to our innermost being. This voice, the voice of God, is the central theme of *Sacred Echoes*. This book stands as a testament to how profoundly and transformationally God's voice has touched my life.

However, *Sacred Echoes* isn't solely about looking back; it's about moving forward with a renewed sense of purpose and a deeper connection with God. It extends an invitation to listen for the echoes of God's voice in our daily lives, urging us to seek His presence amid our everyday struggles and joys. It reminds us that His voice is not distant but ever near. As we embark on this book journey, may you come to recognize how God's voice has echoed throughout your own life. May you find inspiration, comfort, and clarity within the sacred echoes of the past, and may your heart be open to hear His voice speaking to you in the present.

Our lives have a sound, a unique melody that resonates through the corridors of time. It is in the laughter that rings through joyful moments and the tears that fall during times of sorrow. It is in the quiet moments of reflection and the recasting of our daily routines. But it is when God speaks through our lives that the echoes become earnest. His voice weaves through the fabric of our existence. In those moments, our life transforms into a vessel for His message, and the echoes of His wisdom, love, and guidance ripple far and wide. These echoes are not just for us; they touch the hearts of others, leaving an indelible mark. They inspire, console, and uplift. They remind us that our life, with all its ebbs and flows, serves a greater purpose—a purpose that travels through eternity.

Scripture reminds us that even in our moments of weakness when we feel consumed by life's challenges, God's compassion remains unfaltering. Each day is a fresh opportunity for grace and renewal, a testament to the great faithfulness of God. Through life's echoes, the trials and tribulations that test our resolve, we can look back and discern the promises of God. It is in the echoes of our struggles that we perceive the contours of His goodness, the boundless wellspring of His grace, and the depths of His love for us. These echoes, like the sacred resonance of a timeless truth, affirm that we are not alone in our journeys.

As you read these verses and reflect on your own experiences, may you find comfort in the echoes of God's promises, and may you discover that even in the most challenging moments of life, His goodness, grace, and love are ever-present, waiting to be heard and felt. In the chapters that follow, we will delve into stories of individuals, including myself, who have encountered these echoes in impactful ways, illuminating the path towards spiritual growth and deeper connection with the sacred. So, let us continue this book journey guided by the echoes of faith and the promise of a love that knows no bounds. In the vibrant mosaic of faith, God reveals Himself through many names, each carrying a unique essence and meaning.

The name "Adam" has biblical significance and is derived from the Hebrew word "Adamah," which means "earth" or "ground." According to the Bible, in the book of Genesis, Adam was the first man created by God. The name reflects the fact that God formed Adam from the dust of the earth: "Then the Lord God formed the man of dust from the ground and breathed into his nostrils the breath of life, and the man became a living creature" Genesis 2:7. In this context, the name Adam can be seen as a symbolic representation of humanity's earthly origin. It underscores the intimate connection between humanity and the physical world, as well as the idea that human beings were formed by the creative act of God.

Eve has biblical significance as well, and it is associated with the first woman, the wife of Adam, in the book of Genesis. The name Eve is derived from the Hebrew word "Chavah," which means "life" or "living." According to the Bible, Eve was created by God as a companion for Adam "So the Lord God caused a deep sleep to fall upon the man, and while he slept took one of his ribs and closed up its place with flesh. And the rib that the Lord God had taken from the man he made into a woman and brought her to the man. Then the man said, 'This at last is bone of my bones and flesh of my flesh; she shall be called Woman because she was taken out of Man'" Genesis 2:21-23. The name Eve, therefore, carries the meaning of "living" or "life-giver," emphasizing the significance of the first woman as the mother of all living beings.

The seeds of choice and consequence

Let us look back to the dawn of creation, to a garden where the seeds of choice and consequence were sown. The story of Adam and Eve in the Garden of Eden serves as a metaphorical tapestry woven with threads of free will, obedience, and the echoes of God's presence. In the garden, God created Adam and Eve, our primal ancestors, in His image. He placed them in a paradise, providing for their every need and giving them the precious gift of free will. He also placed before them the Tree of Knowledge of Good and Evil along with a singular command, "You may eat from any tree in the garden except the Tree of the Knowledge of Good and Evil. If you eat its fruit, you are sure to die." The question often arises: Why would God place this tree in their midst, knowing the consequences of disobedience? The answer lies in the deep concept of free will. Just as I, as a parent, have expectations for my children but grant them the choice to obey or disobey, God bestowed upon Adam and Eve the power of choice.

Imagine a parent who lovingly prepares a feast for their child, setting a delectable dessert on the table along with a gentle admonition not to indulge in it until after dinner. The dessert, in this metaphor, represents the Tree of Knowledge of Good and

Evil. The parent's instruction is clear, but the choice to obey or disobey lies within the child. In the same way, God's placement of the tree in the garden was an invitation to choose obedience over disobedience, trust over doubt, and faith over curiosity. It was a testament to the nature of free will—the power to make choices that shape our destiny. As we reflect on this metaphor, we come to understand that God's desire was not to impose rigid control but to foster a genuine, heartfelt relationship built on trust and obedience. The tree, like the dessert on the table, was a symbol of His love, trust, and respect for His creation.

We have all faced our own metaphorical trees of choice, moments when the echoes of our decisions reverberated through our lives. We will explore how these choices, whether in obedience or disobedience, shaped our spiritual journeys and illuminated our paths to a deeper connection. We should be mindful of the choices we make, the echoes they create, and the precious nature of free will—a gift that empowers us to choose, to learn, and to grow on our spiritual journey.

As we journey from the pristine garden of Eden, where Adam and Eve grappled with the weight of choice and consequence, we find ourselves stepping into a vastly different landscape—a desolate wilderness where Moses would emerge as a pivotal figure in the unfolding of humanity's relationship with the Creator. The transition from the idyllic perfection of Eden to the harsh realities of the wilderness mirrors the winding paths of our own human experiences where trials and choices intersect with the enduring presence of God.

Moses, a central figure in the biblical narrative, was marked by divine intentionality from the very beginning of his life. His journey, marked by a series of unexpected diversions and changes, serves as a testament to God's plan and presence. The story begins in the land of Egypt, where the Israelites had become a thriving community, causing apprehension among the rulers. Pharaoh, the mighty king, issued a cruel decree that every male Hebrew child born should be cast into the river and left to perish. It was a dark time for the Israelites as the cries of despair echoed across the land. Amid this grim backdrop, a baby boy was born to an Israelite family.

For the first three months of his life, Moses had been hidden in his mother's home because she saw something special in him. Even at his birth, he was regarded as extraordinary due to God's plan. Fearful for their son's life, his parents made a courageous decision—they would place him in a small, waterproof basket and set it afloat in the river's current. They knew that their actions were the only way to preserve their child's life in the face of Pharaoh's despotism. It was a heart-wrenching moment when the basket gently glided along the reeds, carrying the infant away from his family.

When Moses was set afloat in the river, his sister watched from a distance, curious about his fate. Pharaoh's daughter happened to come to the river to bathe and discovered the little ark with the crying baby inside. She was moved by compassion and decided to help. Moses's sister, seizing the moment, suggested that she find a nurse for the baby, and Pharaoh's daughter agreed. The odds seemed insurmountable, and the future appeared bleak. But here, in this seemingly hopeless situation, God's echoes of destiny began to resound. The very daughter of the man who had ordered the death of newly born Hebrew males now sought to preserve this child's life. As the story goes, she eventually brought Moses's own mother to nurse him, and she was even paid to do so. This illustrates a powerful point: We need to entrust our children or loved ones to God and let go of our worries.

Not only did Pharaoh's daughter show compassion, but she also displayed a remarkable willingness to follow God's guiding hand. Instead of adhering to her father's cruel decree, she decided to keep the baby and raise him as her own. Similar to how Moses was set adrift in the river, we too can put our concerns in the ark of prayer and release them into the river of God, where we can find peace, joy, and comfort. It is a call to trust God with our worries and see what He can do. This extraordinary turn of events reveals the powerful hand of God, orchestrating circumstances to protect and raise up Moses as a leader and deliverer of His people.

From the moment Moses was placed in the basket to the day he stood before Pharaoh to demand the release of the Israelites, Moses' life was marked by the echoes of divine providence. The story of Moses reminds us that even in the darkest of times, God's intentions for our lives are sure and purposeful. He intricately blends the strands of our existence into His design, making a way when there seems to be no way. Just as Moses was saved, nurtured, and eventually called to fulfill a mighty purpose, so too can we trust in the echoes of God's guidance in our own lives, knowing that His plan is both detailed and intentional.

As the story of Moses unfolds, he grows up in Pharaoh's household but eventually defends a Hebrew and kills an Egyptian. He is seen in the act and flees for his life to the land of

Midian, a foreign land, and later marries one of the daughters of the priest of Midian. In Egypt, the king dies, and the Israelites, who had been in bondage, begin to cry out to God. He hears their cries and is reminded of the covenant He made with Abraham, Isaac, and Jacob. God looks upon the children of Israel with favor and delivers them. Just as He loved and delivered the children of Israel, He loves and stands ready to deliver us. Simply follow Him to the challenges ahead, and He will, once again, perform miracles, opening a way for you to move forward.

Moses led his father-in-law's flock to a remote desert area, and as the Scriptures recount, he reached the mountain of God. It was during this time that God's love for His people and His willingness to heed their cries became evident. In the pages of the Bible, it is recounted that on the backside of that arid desert, an angel of the Lord appeared to Moses within a burning bush that remained unconsumed by the flames. This sight intrigued Moses, leading him to approach the burning bush to investigate further. From within the midst of the bush, God spoke to him, instructing him to remove his sandals because the ground upon which he stood was considered holy.

Exodus 3:2-15 2 And the angel of the Lord appeared unto him in a flame of fire out of the midst of a bush: and he looked, and, behold, the bush burned with fire, and the bush was not consumed.3 And Moses said, I will now turn aside, and see this great sight, why the bush is not burnt. 4 And when the Lord saw that he turned aside to see, God called unto him out of the midst of the bush, and said, Moses, Moses. And he said, here am I. 5 And he said, draw not nigh hither: put off thy shoes from off thy feet, for the place whereon thou standest is holy ground. 6 Moreover, he said, I am the God of thy father, the God of Abraham, the God of Isaac, and the God of Jacob. And Moses hid his face, for he was afraid to look upon God. 7 And the Lord said, I have surely seen the affliction of my people which are in Egypt, and have heard their cry by reason of their taskmasters; for I know their sorrows; 8 And I am come down to deliver them out of the hand of the Egyptians, and to bring them up out of that land unto a good land and a large, unto a land flowing with milk and honey; unto the place of the Canaanites, and the Hittites, and the Amorites, and the Perizzites, and the Hivites, and the Jebusites. 9 Now therefore, behold, the cry of the children of Israel is come unto me: and I have also seen the oppression wherewith the Egyptians oppress them.10 Come now therefore, and I will send thee unto Pharaoh, that thou mayest bring forth my people the children of Israel out of Egypt. 11 And Moses said unto God, Who am I, that I should go unto Pharaoh, and that I should bring forth the children of Israel out of Egypt? 12 And he said, Certainly I will be with thee, and this shall be a token unto thee, that I have sent thee: When thou hast brought forth the people out of Egypt, ye shall serve God upon this mountain. 13 And Moses said unto God, Behold, when I come unto the children of Israel, and shall say unto them, The God of your fathers hath sent me unto you; and they shall say to me, What is his name? What shall I say unto them? 14 And God said unto Moses, I Am That I Am: and he said, Thus shalt thou say unto the children of Israel, I Am hath sent me unto you. 15 And God said moreover unto Moses, Thus shalt thou say unto the children of Israel, the Lord God of your fathers, the God of Abraham, the God of Isaac, and the God of Jacob, hath sent me unto you: this is my name for ever, and this is my memorial unto all generations.

God revealed Himself as the God of Moses' forefathers—Abraham, Isaac, and Jacob. In that sacred moment, the Lord conveyed that He had seen the suffering of His people in Egypt, heard their cries as they endured oppression, and comprehended the depths of their sorrows. He announced His purpose to deliver them from the clutches of Egypt and guide them to a land abundant with blessings, a land flowing with milk and honey.

God selected Moses for the pivotal role of confronting Pharaoh and leading His people out of their bondage. God provided reassurance, affirming that Moses was the chosen vessel for His divine plan and promising to be with him every step of the way.

Furthermore, God foretold that once Moses had liberated the Israelites from their bondage, they would gather to worship Him on that very mountain. The Moses whom God sent was not an ordinary individual. Instead, he was a divinely appointed messenger entrusted with receiving God's guidance. God's intention was clear: the children of Israel were to follow Moses or face grave consequences, including perishing at the banks of the Red Sea or wandering aimlessly in the wilderness until meeting their end at the Jordan River shores.

As the narrative of Moses demonstrates, being chosen for a momentous task often involves facing daunting challenges and navigating through periods of intense uncertainty. Similarly, the journey I embarked upon following my diagnosis of third-stage thyroid cancer mirrored this biblical trajectory. Moses' path through the desert, marked by trials and divine guidance, finds a reflection in my own struggle against illness. Just as Moses was tasked with leading the Israelites through the wilderness, my diagnosis thrust me into an uncharted territory of medical treatments and emotional turmoil.

I received a diagnosis of third-stage thyroid cancer, a moment that seemed to alter the course of my life dramatically. Much like Moses, who found himself in a vast and desolate desert, I felt isolated and confronted by a landscape of uncertainty. My health condition required radiation iodine treatments, which meant extended periods of separation from my children—a hardship that weighed heavily on my heart. Multiple doctor visits and the physical toll of treatment led to additional health complications, creating a whirlwind of medical challenges. I experienced a persistent sense of fatigue, exhaustion, and overwhelm, as if I were wandering aimlessly through my own personal wilderness. I felt emotionally drained and numb, struggling to find a sense of purpose or direction.

Memory lapses became a daily struggle, forcing me to rely on notes and reminders just to recall basic details. The relentless tiredness made even the simplest tasks feel like monumental feats, and my body went through visible changes, adding to the emotional strain. Adding to the complexity of the situation, I faced vocal cord issues, which disrupted my ability to communicate effectively.

In the midst of speaking, my voice would betray me, faltering mid-sentence, causing my thoughts to scatter like leaves in a gust of wind. This frustrating predicament not only hindered my interactions with others but also intensified the feelings of despair that had firmly rooted within me. Suppose the simple act of expression had become a battle. During this period, I had been asked to speak at various events, including those for cancer survivors and church gatherings. Yet, much like Moses who famously questioned, "Who am I that I should go?" when called upon by God, I too found myself grappling with self-doubt. I questioned my own ability and wondered if I could truly inspire and uplift others in my condition. As you might imagine, these compound challenges exacted an emotional toll.

I can empathize with the frustrations of the children of Israel on their journey to freedom, for each new year has brought me a fresh health challenge. I was exhausted. Depression became an unwelcome companion, a relentless shadow that seemed to shroud every aspect of my life. There were moments when the weight of it all felt insurmountable, and hope appeared as distant as a flickering star in an infinite night sky. In the deepest depths of my struggle, however, I held onto the recognition that I needed to summon the same wellspring of resilience that Moses exemplified during his sojourn in the wilderness. It became clear that I could not succumb to the despair that sought to consume me. Instead, I had to continue fighting, nurturing the firm belief that hope endured even in the darkest moments.

With steadfast determination and the passage of time, I clung to the conviction that things would indeed improve. I dared to envision a future bathed in a brighter, more promising light. I asked God to open the eyes of my heart to change the way I see things. I want to always have my eyes and my mind fixed on Him. I want to see Him in every situation in my life. Just as Moses found his way through the wilderness and ultimately fulfilled his divine purpose, I too began to see progress in my journey. Incrementally, I regained my strength, my voice, and my sense of purpose, proving that even in the most challenging of times, I could find a path forward.

In Galatians 6:9, we are reminded, "And let us not grow weary of doing good, for in due season we will reap if we do not give up." There are moments in life when giving up feels like the most straightforward path. Countless obstacles can stand in the way of our perseverance, hindering our progress and preventing us from reaching the place God has set for us. I realize that oftentimes, I am the biggest obstacle to my own progress. I have let external circumstances, challenging situations, and even my own thoughts dishearten me. Regrettably, I have sometimes settled into this discouragement so deeply that it paved the way for negative influences to convince me to abandon my path.

During these moments of solitude and reflection, I often recall how God managed to capture Moses's attention on the backside of that very desert. In a similar fashion, during my own period of isolation, I sensed a shift in my life. It was as if God, in His divine wisdom, chose this moment to seize my attention and initiate a meaningful conversation with me. For the first time in my life, amid the stillness of comfort, I began to grasp the depth of His presence. It was in these moments of quiet contemplation that I discovered there were far more significant and meaningful pursuits in life than the endless chase after worldly desires and ambitions.

God unleashed a series of plagues upon Egypt, eventually softening the hardened heart of Pharaoh. This change of heart led to a pivotal moment—the release of the Israelites from their long-standing bondage. As they set forth on their journey towards the Promised Land, they found themselves navigating the vast wilderness. However, their path was soon blocked by an apparently insurmountable obstacle—the Red Sea. Pharaoh had a change of heart once again and dispatched his chariots to recapture the Israelites, leaving them trapped between the sea and the rapidly approaching Egyptian army. In this dire moment, God, in His boundless mercy and omnipotence, orchestrated a miraculous event. Through the outstretched staff of Moses, He commanded the Red Sea to part its waters, creating a miraculous pathway amidst the sea.

With great relief and gratitude, the Israelites embarked on this path, with towering walls of water standing on either side. However, as the last Israelite safely reached the opposite shore, the pursuing Egyptian army recklessly charged into the divided waters. Just as swiftly as the sea had parted, it came crashing down upon the Egyptians, engulfing Pharaoh's forces in a watery demise. The Israelites were at last free from the oppressive grasp of Egypt. Their hearts brimming with gratefulness and awe, Moses and the Israelites erupted in a jubilant song of praise to God for this astounding deliverance.

This anthem, known as the "Song of Moses," resonated throughout the wilderness, serving as an enduring testament to their faith and gratitude. Having broken free from the chains of Egyptian tyranny, the Israelites continued their journey, guided by the ever-present hand of God. Along the way, they encountered fresh challenges, but in their time of need, God faithfully provided. He sent down manna, a mysterious sustenance from the heavens, to nourish them. Additionally, He granted them quail for sustenance and miraculously provided water from a rock to quench their thirst, all of which attested to His unceasing care and provision.

Their journey eventually led them to Mount Sinai, a place where Moses received not only the Ten Commandments but also the Law of God. During Moses' time on the mountain, however, some of the people grew impatient and crafted a golden calf, turning away from the worship of the Almighty. It was a moment of great sin, but Moses interceded on their behalf, seeking God's forgiveness, which was graciously granted. Following this, God supplied explicit instructions for the construction of the Tabernacle, a portable sanctuary intended to house His divine presence among the people. Yet, as their journey unfolded, it was not without its trials. Upon reaching the borders of the Promised Land, they decided to send twelve spies to scout the territory. Regrettably, driven by fear and disbelief, most of the spies returned with a discouraging report.

This report instilled doubt and hesitation among the people, leading to dire consequences. God decreed that they would wander in the wilderness for forty long years until the faithless generation had passed away. During this period, leadership transitioned from Moses to Joshua, who would ultimately guide the Israelites into the long-awaited Promised Land. Upon the culmination of the forty years of wandering, a new generation stood poised on the banks of the Jordan River, prepared to embark on their journey into Canaan. Under Joshua's capable leadership, they successfully crossed the river, embarking on the monumental task of conquering the Promised Land.

This endeavor was not without its share of battles and challenges as they diligently worked to claim the territory God had promised them. The overarching narrative of the Israelites' journey was characterized by God's resolute guidance, His generous provision, His necessary discipline, and His consistent faithfulness. Throughout their travels from Egypt to the Promised Land, they gleaned invaluable lessons about the importance of obedience, trust, and the enduring relationship they shared with God—not merely obedience to Moses but, above all, obedience to the God whose voice resonated through him." During the arduous journey of leading the Israelites out of Egypt and towards the Promised Land, it was striking to notice how they often found themselves entangled in complaints about various adversities.

They seemed to focus on everything that went wrong, creating doubt, instead of keeping faith in the same God who had delivered them and His ability to do it once more. Their grumbling and discontent mirrored my own experiences during the years of recovery from thyroid cancer. I encountered one health challenge after another, each adding to the weight of my struggle. Thyroid cancer was only the beginning. I also had to confront PCOS (Polycystic Ovary Syndrome), a condition that presented its own set of challenges. Then came the unexpected need for gallbladder removal, as doctors initially believed it was the source of my discomfort, only to discover that it was gastroparesis, a condition affecting my stomach's ability to function properly.

Moreover, I underwent two hernia surgeries, and it felt like my body was consistently in a state of turmoil. Fatigue, both physical and emotional, became my constant companion. Like the Israelites in the wilderness, I found myself complaining about the relentless challenges life had thrown my way. As if the load were not heavy enough, there was yet another twist in the plot.

My doctor contacted me after a routine checkup and informed me that I needed another radioactive iodine treatment.

Despite no longer having a thyroid, a small residual issue had been detected on my scar tissue. The doctors decided against surgical removal, fearing that doing so might lead to its spread within the scar tissue. Instead, they opted to watch it closely and treat it as needed. This revelation was yet another source of anxiety and complaint. I was so absorbed in what was seemingly going wrong with my body that I momentarily lost sight of the most essential truth—my Father is a healer.

During it all, I had to undergo another radioactive iodine treatment. During my treatment, I had to undergo another session of radioactive iodine therapy. This necessitated a period of strict isolation, a protocol essential for the safety of others. Radioactive iodine, while effective in targeting thyroid cancer cells, emits radiation that can be harmful to those around me. As a result, patients such as myself are required to stay in a separate room, limiting contact with family, friends, and even healthcare staff to a minimum. This isolation is not just a physical separation but also a precautionary measure to prevent the transfer of radiation to others. It's a solitary phase, where one's own body temporarily becomes a source of potential risk to loved ones, necessitating this period of solitude for their protection.

It was during this solitude that I shifted my focus. I turned to prayer, dedicated time to studying and understanding His word, poured my thoughts and feelings into journaling, and cherished the moments spent with God. This period of separation became an intense spiritual journey—a time to strengthen my faith and reaffirm my belief in His healing power. In the end, the challenges and trials served as a reminder that, just like the Israelites, I needed to focus on the unchanging faithfulness of my Heavenly Father, who had delivered me in the past and remained my constant source of hope and healing.

Through the trials of my health journey, I discovered a connection with the words of Isaiah 57:18-19 "I have seen their ways, but I will heal them; I will guide them and restore comfort to Israel's mourners, creating praise on their lips. Peace, peace, to those far and near,' says the Lord, 'and I will heal them." These verses took on a new dimension of meaning in my life. They became more than just words; they were a testament to the transformative power of God's healing touch. My journey through various ailments allowed me to intimately know God as a healer, not just of my body but of my soul. During physical challenges, I found spiritual healing and restoration. The promise of peace resonated not only with my body but with my spirit, bringing comfort and praise to my lips.

Through it all, I learned that God's healing extends beyond the physical, reaching into the depths of our souls, offering comfort, renewal, and a sense of His presence. As I reflect on the stories of Adam and Eve in the garden and the epic journey of Moses through the wilderness, I see a common thread that weaves through both narratives—the human experience of trials, choices, and the unchanging nature of God. Just as Adam and Eve faced the choice of obedience or disobedience in the garden, and just as Moses confronted the daunting challenges of leading the Israelites to the Promised Land, we, too, encounter our own moments of decision and struggle. These stories are a testament to the enduring themes of free will, redemption, and the faithfulness of the Almighty. They remind us that even in our moments of weakness and doubt, God's love and grace are steadfast, offering hope and guidance on our unique journeys of faith.

Today, I find myself attuned to echoes emanating from the very burning bush where God first spoke to Moses. The flame of God continues to convey its message. Despite the vast expanse of time, God's communication endures, conveyed through the fire and the indwelling Spirit. Just as God loved the children of Israel, He loves us. And just as He delivered them, He is waiting to deliver us. Whenever we congregate in His divine presence, and the Spirit stirs among us, we find ourselves standing upon the sacred ground—a place where wonder-working Power lives. From the burning bush, God dispatches these echoing messages, signaling that His people are still in bondage- their cries reaching His compassionate ears. He has paved the way, and now He summons us to proclaim His truth to this present generation, beseeching that their eyes may be unveiled to the truth and their ears unstoppered to hear His word. The constancy of God remains unaltered. He persists in His divine attributes, unwavering.

Dawna Lindsey

AN ECHO THAT LINGERS

During my formative years, I observed my parents grappling with the weight of childhood trauma, marital struggles, the pressures of adulthood, and the inherent anxieties of raising a family. At that time, I failed to fully appreciate the depth of their challenges. However, as I have grown older, I have come to not only appreciate but also deeply admire their commitment. Regardless of the hardships they faced, one constant remained: they consistently kept our family rooted in the church. Looking back, I now realize the significance of this decision and the impact it had on our lives. I used to tell myself that when I grew older, I would not be as committed to going to church as my parents were. We were in church every Wednesday, Friday, and

Sunday, and as a child, it felt like a lot. But now that I am older, I find that my heart longs for that fellowship and spiritual connection.

I have come to realize that the foundation my parents laid during my childhood has become an essential part of who I am today. The values, faith, and sense of community I gained from those church gatherings are irreplaceable, and I am grateful for the legacy my parents passed down to me. As I reflect on their complete dedication, I pray that one day, the echoes of their efforts to keep me grounded in the Lord will linger down to my own children, creating a generational legacy of faith and steadfastness. My siblings and I did not have the privilege of growing up under the same roof, and as a result, we all carry our own unique challenges stemming from our childhoods. I recognize and appreciate that our parents, like everyone else, had their own struggles and issues to contend with. It is a reality that when we do not confront and address these challenges, they can often become generational, passing down from one generation to the next.

Before my mom began attending church, our lives were marked by the shadow of addiction. I witnessed and experienced things that I wish I could erase from my memory. Those were dark days, and hope felt like a distant star in the night sky. My mother's battle with addiction was a journey fraught with pain, chaos, and despair. The grip of substances had taken hold of her, leading our family down a treacherous path. It was a world filled with uncertainty, fear, and heartbreak. However, a remarkable transformation occurred as my mother began her journey toward deliverance. It was like seeing a phoenix rising from the ashes, a beacon of hope amidst the darkness. The church became a sanctuary of healing and redemption, a place where my mother's spirit was revived, and her soul found freedom. The transition from addiction to deliverance was not without its challenges.

Sobriety requires immense courage, determination, and faith. It was a testament to the power of love, community, and the divine grace able to mend even the most broken of spirits. As I reflect on those transformative moments, I am reminded of the boundless ability for change and renewal that lives within each of us. My mother's journey serves as a powerful reminder that, no matter how deep the pit, there is always a path to restoration and deliverance. It is a story of hope, resilience, and the enduring power of faith to conquer even the darkest of circumstances.

Despite the loving guidance of my parents and the nurturing environment of our church, there were moments in my life that caused fear, doubt, and worry to creep in. It was as if these unwelcome guests lurked in the shadows, waiting for the right opportunity to surface. Abandonment and self-guilt often went with these feelings. I questioned whether I was truly worthy of love and belonging. I wrestled with the thought of being left behind or cast aside by those I held dear. The weight of self-doubt hung heavily on my shoulders, eroding my faith and confidence. Each struggle was a proclamation that faith is not immune to the storms of life.

Even in the most nurturing of environments, we may still confront moments of uncertainty and vulnerability. I recall one of those moments at a particular church outing. The church had taken the youth to an event where we were gathered at a pool. During this event, one of the older guys decided to playfully pick me up and toss me into the pool. Little did he know that moment would unlock a deep-seated fear of water within me, as I had no prior experience with swimming. At first glance, my fear of water stemming from a seemingly insignificant incident might not appear to hold much significance in the grand scheme of things. However, you will come to recognize the intentional hand of God at work. This particular event marked the onset of my lifelong struggle with fear, making it a pivotal moment in my journey that would go on to shape many aspects of my life, influencing decisions, reactions, and even my faith. It serves as a testament to how seemingly small incidents can have a significant impact, especially when viewed through the lens of faith and personal growth. As we delve deeper into my story, remember that even the most seemingly insignificant experiences have carried significant meaning in the larger fabric of my life.

From my earliest memories of my life, where the fear of water gripped me, to the weighty experiences that would follow, I began to understand how fear could shape a person's journey. Just as my fear of water seemed insignificant at the time but would later reveal its impact on my life, in the story of Tamar (2 Samuel 13), in this narrative, we encounter the consequences of a series of seemingly mundane choices that spiral into a heart-wrenching family tragedy. It is a stark reminder that even the smallest of actions and decisions can have far-reaching implications, much like the ripples caused by a stone tossed into a calm pond. The exploration of Tamar's story uncovers the echoes of pain, betrayal, and ultimately, the pursuit of justice in the midst of complex family dynamics.

In 2 Samuel 13, we are confronted with the sobering reality of how sin can insidiously infiltrate and corrupt even the most sacred relationships, leaving behind a trail of destruction and shattered lives. This chapter serves as a poignant reminder of the critical and lasting impact sin can have on individuals and families. The roots of this tragic story can be traced back to the grievous sins committed by David, the great king of Israel. His illicit affair with Bathsheba and the subsequent treacherous murder of her husband, Uriah, were the initial acts that set-in motion a chain of events leading to the calamity we witness in 2 Samuel 13. David's moral failure and misguided attempts to cover up his wrongdoing created a festering wound in the texture of his family. The corrosive nature of sin left unchecked poisons the atmosphere within the household. It breeds an atmosphere of mistrust, jealousy, and vengeance, ultimately driving a wedge between family members who should have been united in love and support.

Instead, we see the heartbreaking tragedy of Amnon's heinous actions toward his half-sister Tamar and Absalom's revenge-fueled response. In the annals of David's tumultuous family, a disturbing and tragic episode unfolds, centered on his son, Amnon, and his half-sister, Tamar. While the text initially labels Amnon's emotions as 'love,' it becomes painfully clear that this was no selfless, sacrificial love but rather a consuming and destructive lust driven by personal desires. Amnon's intentions are far from pure, and his actions ultimately lead to the rape of his sister. Amnon's sinister plot takes shape with the aid of his friend Jonadab, as they craft a cunning scheme that cunningly enlists King David's unwitting cooperation. Under the guise of illness, Amnon manipulates his father into summoning Tamar to tend to him. Once she arrives, Amnon dismisses her objections and perpetrates a heinous act of violation.

In the wake of this horrifying transgression, Amnon's heart undergoes a chilling transformation. His supposed 'love' for Tamar turns to loathing, and he ruthlessly casts her aside. Tamar, left shattered and grieving over her ordeal, finds support in her brother Absalom. Absalom appears as a beacon of decency amidst the darkness that shrouds their family. He offers comfort to Tamar and takes her into his care. Yet, the weight of the assault bears heavily on him. The text reveals that Absalom harbors a seething hatred for Amnon, a festering grudge that simmers beneath the surface for an extended period, setting the stage for further turmoil within this fractured family. As we reflect on this narrative, it serves as a solemn cautionary about the enduring consequences of sin. It underscores the importance of acknowledging our transgressions, seeking repentance and forgiveness, and striving for reconciliation with God and one another. The repercussions of sin may linger for generations, but the hope of redemption and healing is always within reach when we turn to God with contrite hearts.

When I was a teenager, my world was shaken by the separation of my parents. It was a time of confusion and emotional turmoil. My mom, who had always been hardworking, found herself spending increased time away from home. Meanwhile, my dad, who had also been a significant presence in my life, seemed to drift away. It was a difficult period for me, and I could not understand why my dad was not there for me when I needed him the most. As I reflect on those days now, I realize that his absence was not a matter of choice but a consequence of circumstances. Life can be complex, and sometimes, it forces people down paths they never intended to take. My dad's physical absence during that time did not diminish the love and care he had for me. It was simply a challenging chapter in our family's story.

Life thrust upon me an unexpected and challenging role. I had to learn the intricacies of cooking and caring for others at an age when most kids were focused on simpler pursuits. It felt like an overwhelming responsibility and an immense pressure, one that was difficult to bear at times. However, in the crucible of those formative years, my character was being molded, and the seeds of nurturing were being sown. Little did I know that these early challenges would become the cornerstone of my character.

Through the challenges of those years, I discovered my innate ability to nurture and care for those around me. The echoes of those experiences resonate throughout my life to this day. They instilled in me a profound sense of empathy, teaching me to put others' needs before my own. They forged my resilience, enabling me to navigate life's hurdles with determination. They molded me into a woman who understands the power of compassion and the beauty of selflessness.

Despite my parents' separation, I felt a keen sense of responsibility for my family. Taking care of my younger siblings was something that came naturally to me. I made sure my siblings were fed, looked after their homework, and ensured they were unharmed. My mom, even though she was often away, still wanted to ensure our well-being. She found a babysitter to come and check on us from time to time just to be certain that we were okay. One day was not okay. The babysitter left us and walked to her house, which was just a street over from ours. I was home, taking a nap in my room. As I slept, a pillow covered my head.

Someone forced my head down into the pillow. My pants were pulled down. Someone brushed up against me.

I felt so helpless and abandoned. I had no one to help. The babysitter returned. When she began to beat on the door, he got off of me and walked out as if nothing ever happened. I was numb! I asked the babysitter to keep quiet about it, too. The reason for my silence was that I did not want my dad to find out and potentially react in a harmful way. One of my brothers was already in and out of trouble. Another brother was focused on getting his life together. Plus, I had not yet developed a close relationship with my other brothers. Despite my deep connection with my grandaddy, I did not believe he could handle such news. I did not want to disrupt anyone's life, especially because this kind of thing had happened so many times in my family, and it seemed like no one ever took action or made a difference. I decided to carry that heavy burden silently. As a result, I was constantly getting into physical fights. I started living a wild and carefree life. I even began to question my sexuality.

I had so many perversive thoughts, and although I never acted on those thoughts, they were there, confusing and troubling me. I could not understand why I was having these feelings or where they were coming from. To find comfort and escape the pain, I got involved in various activities, but none of them supplied the relief I desperately looked for. I remained numb and deeply hurting. In my own harrowing experience with a trusted family member, I find a deep resonance with Tamar. While our situations differ – in my case, the betrayal came not from a brother but from someone else deeply trusted within the family – the emotional landscape we navigated is strikingly similar. Tamar, betrayed by her own brother, must have been overwhelmed with guilt and shame, a feeling I can empathize with deeply. Like Tamar, who faced a great violation within the supposed safety of her family, I too, struggled with the repercussions of being wronged by someone my parents and I trusted. Our experiences, though separated by time and context, share the themes of betrayal. We both had to find our way in a world that often overlooks such deep personal traumas.

I had knowledge of God, but He felt incredibly distant. I found myself questioning His very existence and wrestling with the "why" – why would He allow all these painful things to happen to me? The pain and confusion ran so deep that I couldn't help but wonder if God was truly there, and if He was, why He seemed so far away during my moments of need. It was a period of great doubt and questioning that I could not easily work through. Back then, God didn't seem like the loving deity I had heard about. During those trying moments, His love seemed elusive. I could not understand why, if He was a loving God, He would allow me to go through such pain and confusion. As I have grown older and have gained more perspective, I have come to realize that God does not make the world evil; our choices and actions taint it. We have all been given the gift of free will, and it is the choice we make with that free will that often leads to suffering and evil in the world.

Despite the darkness we create, God stays steadfast in His love, His faithfulness, and His justice. It is a lesson I have learned over time. God's love endures, even when our world seems to fall apart. Psalm 68:5 tells us that God is the "Father of the fatherless and protector of widows." Now, this psalm resonates with me on a personal level. I have seen how God's aim is to extend His mercy, care, and protection to those who are vulnerable and in need. It is a reminder that the vulnerable youth, often overlooked by the world, are precious to Him, and as His Church, they should be essential to us as well. The concept of El Roi, the Lord who sees me, from Genesis 16:13, has become a reassurance in my life. I have come to understand that God sees me in all my uniqueness.

Psalm 139:14 further emphasizes that "I am fearfully and wonderfully made by Him." These verses remind me that I am not alone, and God's eyes are always upon me. Deuteronomy 31:8, which assures that the Lord goes before us and will never leave or forsake us, has been a rock of strength during challenging times. It is a promise that I hold onto, knowing that no matter what I face, God is with me, and I need not fear. Lastly, the words of Jesus in Matthew 28:20, where He promises to be with us always, to the end of the age, have become a constant source of hope. It is a reminder that His presence is enduring, and He walks beside us throughout our journey.

Finding comfort in the Bible when going through challenging times is a reassuring and relatable experience. Knowing that you can open the Bible and find stories of people who have faced similar challenges and trusted God to bring them through those trials is a source of strength. It reminds us that we are not alone in our circumstances and that others have walked similar paths with God's guidance and support, ultimately emerging victorious. The Bible serves as a timeless source of encouragement, showing that God's faithfulness extends through generations, offering hope and solace to those who seek it.

I still grapple with the memories of what happened to me, and at times, the pain and anger can be overwhelming. Yet, I have made it a constant practice to bring these feelings before God. There are moments when I was tempted to seek revenge, believing I have every right to do so. However, I am reminded of important Scriptures like "Vengeance is mine, saith the Lord" (Romans 12:19). These words encourage me to trust in God's justice and timing rather than take matters into my own hands. It is a challenging journey, but I have learned to lean on God's guidance and healing rather than seeking revenge or holding on to anger. Every time those painful memories resurface, I find it crucial to forgive, even when it feels incredibly difficult. I have come to realize that harboring anger and resentment only gives those memories more power over me.

I do not want those thoughts to take root and fester in my heart, leading me down a path of bitterness and more pain. So, I choose forgiveness, not just for the ones who may have hurt me but for my own well-being and peace of mind. It is a continuous process, but it is one that helps me prevent anger from taking hold in my heart. During such tumultuous circumstances, it is easy to become deaf to the echoes of love and commitment that persist.

These echoes serve as a reminder that even in the most trying times, we can rise above the darkness and become the people we are meant to be. It is in these moments of crisis that we are confronted with the choice between succumbing to the corrosive effects of anger and revenge or embracing the transformative power of forgiveness and love. While the path toward justice can be arduous, it is essential to keep in mind that seeking retribution often perpetuates a cycle of pain. Instead, we can draw inspiration from the enduring echoes of love, choosing a higher road that leads to healing and restoration.

It is a challenging journey, but one that ultimately brings about the transformation of both individuals and communities, reminding us of the resilience of the human spirit and the potential for redemption, even in the face of the gravest injustices. Anger and grief can be seen as a testament to the depth of our relationships with God, as we turn to Him in times of pain and seek His presence and understanding. Our journey through these emotions can ultimately lead to a deeper and more authentic connection with God, just as David's Psalms did for him. The journey towards transformation, guided by forgiveness and love, reminds us of the significant influence that individuals can have in our lives, shaping our paths and our responses to life's challenges. Just as we choose to rise above anger and grief, turning towards resilience and redemption, I am reminded of a personal embodiment of these virtues – my grandfather.

As long as I can remember, my granddaddy was a deacon in the church. He was a pillar of faith and strength, a man whose small frame belied the giant heart within. To me, he was more than just a grandfather; he was my hero, my voice of reason, and my safe space. His dedication to serving God and holding our family together left an indelible mark on my young heart. After school, as worries of the day would fade, I would eagerly journey to his house. There, under the comforting shelter of the carport, we would share stories, and he would share his green and white peppermints with me. Those simple moments spent in his company were a sanctuary for my soul. I was just 14 years old when I discovered that I was pregnant with my son. The thought of breaking this news to my granddaddy weighed heavily on my heart. I couldn't bear the idea of disappointing him, but to my relief, he was incredibly supportive. He offered me words of wisdom and guidance that would shape my journey into motherhood.

His words to me were, "Make sure he knows the Lord. If you don't do anything else, make sure he knows the Lord." At 15 years old, I gave birth to my son. My granddaddy played an instrumental role in both our lives. He spent precious time with my son, nurturing a bond that would prove to be invaluable. Our visits to my granddaddy's house became a cherished tradition, and my son found comfort in the presence of this remarkable man.

One day, during one of our visits, my granddaddy shared a seemingly unusual request with me. He said, "I want to see this boy with a haircut before I go." I was puzzled because it was our family tradition to wait until a baby's first birthday to cut their hair. I asked him why he felt this way, and he explained to me that death was a natural part of life, something we all must face. It was a conversation that stuck with me, though I couldn't understand its significance at the time.

Unbeknownst to me, this conversation would serve as a poignant foreshadowing of what lay ahead. My granddaddy's words about life and death became hauntingly prescient. Not long after our talk, he passed away. I was unprepared, and the reality of his absence struck me like a thunderbolt. Questions swirled in my mind, and I was filled with a sense of loss. I needed him more than ever, and there were so many things left unsaid, so many conversations left unspoken. My granddaddy's passing marked my first encounter with grief, and I was utterly unprepared for the intensity of the emotions that flooded my heart. I was angry with God, my faith shaken to its core.

How could a man so dear to me, a man of faith, be taken away so soon? The pain was raw, and the void he left in my life felt insurmountable. In my grief, I struggled with the harsh reality of his absence and the unanswered questions that echoed in my heart. But as time would reveal, my granddaddy had been preparing my heart all along, not just for the joy of motherhood but also for the pain of loss. His words about life's inevitable cycle were a reminder that death is an inescapable part of our human journey. Though my mind had tried to convince me that he would live forever, my heart began to understand that he had imparted a valuable lesson in acceptance, even in the face of heart-wrenching sorrow.

In the years that followed the loss of my granddaddy, I would come to realize that his legacy lived on not only in the memories we shared but also in the enduring strength of my faith. Through the depths of my grief and anger, I would learn to find encouragement in the sacred echoes of his wisdom and love that resonated throughout my life. My granddaddy had left me with a precious gift—the understanding that even in the midst of loss, faith could be a source of comfort and resilience, guiding me through the darkest of times.

King David, though described as a man after God's own heart, expressed moments of anger and frustration in the Psalms. He often poured out his heart to God, sharing his struggles, doubts, and fears. There are moments in life when we just can't help but feel angry, frustrated, and lost. It is part of being human, and even King David, a man described as having a heart after God's own, experienced these emotions. In the Psalms, David poured out his heart to God, sharing his raw emotions, struggles, and, yes, even his anger. He did not hold back, and neither should we. It is human to express our doubts, fears, and frustrations to the One who knows us best.

Just like David, we can use our own expressions, whether through writing, worshipping with song, or prayer to process these feelings. And you know what? Our relationship with God is not weakened by our emotions. In fact, it is deepened. Our honesty with Him in moments of pain and loss shows our faith in action. Just as David's Psalms strengthened his connection with God, our journey through anger and grief can lead us to a more meaningful and authentic relationship with the Almighty. So, let us remember it is human to feel, to be angry, and to grieve.

Share it with God because He is always there to listen and provide comfort in times of sorrow.

Dawna Lindsey

ECHOES OF GRIEF AND GRACE

In the depths of our darkest hours, we often find ourselves searching for a reason, for a glimmer of hope to pierce through the shroud of despair. It is in those moments when we are most vulnerable when the weight of our grief threatens to engulf us, that we may come to understand the pain of Mary, the mother of Jesus, who stood at the foot of her son's cross as he suffered and died. Just as she felt the searing agony of loss, I, too, knew the depths of a mother's grief, for I lost my own son. In the pages of the Bible, Mary's anguish is a poignant reminder of the pain that transcends time and culture. Her story resonates with any parent who has endured the indescribable heartache of losing a child. And just as God may have prepared Mary's heart for the death of her son, I, too, felt as though God had been preparing my heart for the unthinkable.

In the books of Matthew, Mark, Luke, and John, it is chronicled that Mary is present at Jesus' crucifixion. It is incredibly difficult to imagine the pain she must have felt, watching her son endure such savage mockery, pain, and torture. Mary stood witness as Jesus was crucified on Golgotha, also known as Calvary, a hill where crucifixions took place publicly— a brutal and agonizing form of execution. Her presence at her son's crucifixion is often seen as a symbol of great sorrow and maternal anguish, representing the suffering experienced by Jesus and his loved ones. In that agonizing moment, Mary dropped to her knees, her grief too heavy to carry. The memory of her son's final cry, as he endured hours of torment, echoed in her ears. The sky had darkened at noon, and the earth shook violently, as described in Matthew 27:45- 51. To Mary, it might have seemed as though even Jehovah himself was expressing deep sorrow over the death of Jesus.

As Jesus spoke seven statements, often called the "Seven Last Words," expressing forgiveness, compassion, and a sense of abandonment, memories from around 33 years earlier likely flooded her mind, including the recollection of when she and

Joseph presented their precious baby at the temple in Jerusalem. At that time, an elderly man named Simeon had prophesied, foretelling wonderful things for Jesus but also warning Mary that one day she would feel as if a sword had pierced her heart (Luke 2:25-35). It was in this tragic hour that she fully understood the truth of those words. Just as Mary experienced a pivotal moment of deep understanding and sorrow, foretold by Simeon's prophecy when witnessing the crucifixion of her son, a similarly transformative period awaited me in my faith journey. In 2015, my path took a significant turn as I embarked on Minister classes, immersed myself further in my Bible studies, prayed with increased fervor, and sought a personal connection with God, not realizing that these steps were fortifying me for an upcoming test of my faith's resilience.

In December of that same year, I received a phone call that would forever alter the course of my life. It was a call that no parent should ever have to receive—my only biological son had been shot. Racing to the scene, I clung to the hope that he might still be alive. As I arrived, my eyes fell upon an ambulance, and for a fleeting moment, I believed my son might be inside, injured but alive. I rushed towards it with trembling hope, only to be met with the cold, unfeeling words of two police officers: "I'm sorry, ma'am, he's deceased." In that instant, my world shattered.

The earth seemed to shift beneath me as grief threatened to consume me whole. I cried out to God, questioning how He could allow this unbearable tragedy to befall me. The police officers stood nearby, their callousness cutting through the silence, as they continued to talk and laugh. I felt invisible, lost, numb, confused... BROKEN.

My younger sister, unable to contain her own anguish and anger at the officers' lack of empathy, erupted in a torrent of tears and curses. It was in this darkest hour that I realized the importance of relying on the strength and peace of God. I needed His support to carry me through the storm that had descended upon my life. As I struggled with the unimaginable pain of losing my son, I questioned everything. I had been doing all the right things—going to church, reading my Bible, praying fervently, and even sharing my faith with others. Yet, in the midst of my faithful journey, I had lost my son.

My heart ached, and my faith was shaken to its core. But in that very moment of despair, God whispered to me words of promise and comfort: "I will destroy the body to save the soul. I make all things new." God's words became my lifeline, my anchor in the tempest of grief. They provided me with the strength and peace I needed to endure what was, and still is, the most painful experience I've ever had to face. I can still hear God's words echoing, a reassuring reminder of His presence and promise in the midst of life's storms.

I clung to His promises, for I knew that only through His grace could I find the strength to stand behind my son's casket and preach a word of hope and faith to those who gathered to mourn. I also thought about my granddaddy's words to me. Words that not only helped me in the process of motherhood but also in my times of grief. I thought he was only preparing my heart for his death, but his words echoed over the years and assisted with the preparation for the death of my own son. I am so grateful that he encouraged me to make sure my son knew God.

In the wake of such deep sorrow, I learned that grief has a way of consuming us if we allow it. It can turn moments of despair into lasting lifestyles of desolation and sorrow. However, I could not get stuck in a quagmire of perpetual grief. I had to process my emotions, surrender them to God, and trust that He would continue to heal and comfort me. In my moments of overwhelming sorrow, when hurt, anger and grief threatened to drown me, I learned to call upon the name of Jesus. I had to turn to God and allow Him to be the sovereign ruler over my emotions.

The memories of my son, his life, and his impact on others have become a source of comfort and joy. After his passing, his classmates, friends, and adults who had known him shared stories of how he had touched their lives. He was remembered as a young man full of love, wisdom, and forgiveness. His school planted a tree in his honor, a symbol of the enduring impact he had on the lives of those he touched. In the aisles of a grocery store, a woman approached me, recognizing me as Trevon's mother. She asked for a hug and shared how my son had protected her child from a bully at school. My son is a protector. Even in the face of unimaginable loss, I felt reassured by the knowledge that my son's legacy lived.

Through my own journey of grief, I have come to understand that life's most meaningful echoes are often born in the depths of our pain. Just as Mary's presence at her son's crucifixion bore witness to the depths of maternal love and anguish, my own experiences have shown me that God's grace is sufficient, even in the darkest of hours. I have learned to listen to the sacred echoes that resonate throughout my life, guiding me through the most challenging times.

A few months after my son's passing, I received a phone call from a friend. He was speaking to a girl who had experienced the heartbreaking loss of her baby right in her arms. He admitted to me, "I don't know what to say to her because I've never experienced that, but I told her I knew someone who could help her." I agreed to call her back, but I needed a couple of days to pray about it. I didn't want my words to come from my own emotions. Our own emotions and feelings can often lead us astray; however, I passionately believe that we can never go wrong when we allow the Holy Spirit to take control.

I called her. I first apologized for the delay, explaining that I had to pray about it. She shared with me the tragic story of her baby's passing, but what struck me most was when she said that she saw her baby every night in her dreams. She confessed that she hated waking up because she longed to spend time with her baby in those dreams. I couldn't help but ask her a question that had been weighing on my heart:

"Do you think God would take the very thing that's causing you so much pain and dangle it in front of you every night?" I firmly believe that God desires to comfort us, not torment us. He longs for us to come to Him, broken, angry, and confused, so that He can do the healing work that needs to be done. As the psalmist wrote, "God is close to the brokenhearted and saves those who are crushed in spirit" (Psalm 34:18). God wants to be our refuge and our resting place. I shared with her a personal experience I had endured.

For a week straight, I had the same dream every night. In the dream, I was sitting on my couch, and my son walked into the living room, saying, "Momma, I miss you!" In response, I would tell him, "You are gone; I have to bring you back." We would then walk silently to the graveyard, where I would dig up his grave and put him back inside, covering his body once again. This haunting dream tormented me night after night. At the time, I couldn't understand why I was going through this torment while trying to offer encouragement and comfort to someone else. But looking back, I realize that sometimes we must personally experience certain things to truly empathize with and understand what others are going through. I could now testify to the fact that I had been there, and I did understand. Those dreams were not of God. It would have been easy for me to slip into depression if I had allowed myself to find comfort in the dream of seeing my son again rather than relying on God's strength and comfort.

There were times I would look at pictures of my son or just think, "I wonder what he would be like right now." Tears would fall; my head would start spinning; the room started to cave in, and my chest would tighten. It felt like I was drowning in a pool of grief. I did not want to think of him, but sometimes it would hurt, so it was a battle within myself. I would think about him and then try to block the thought out so that I would not fall into that pool. It was a tiresome battle. "Come to me, all you who are weary and burdened, and I will give you rest" (Matthew 11:28). This verse is an invitation from Jesus, offering comfort and rest to those who are tired and burdened by life's challenges. It encourages people to turn to Him for rest and find peace in His presence. I embarked on a journey that went beyond seeking God.

I began to ask God to show me myself, to reveal the depths of my own heart and soul. I did not know that this request would lead me to an earnest and sometimes unsettling exploration of my innermost being. As I rummaged into this journey of self-discovery, I was confronted with aspects of myself that I had long ignored or denied. It was as if God was shining a light into the hidden corners of my heart, illuminating both the beauty and the brokenness within me. Honestly, I didn't always like what I uncovered. I discovered my own vulnerabilities, fears, and insecurities. I confronted the anger and bitterness that had taken root in my soul, stemming from the loss of my son and the other hardships life had thrown my way.

Facing the reality of my imperfections and the need for healing was a raw and uncomfortable process. Yet, through it all, I came to understand that this journey of self-discovery was an essential part of my healing process. It allowed me to acknowledge my pain, my questions, and my doubts and to bring them before God. It was an invitation to lay bare my brokenness and trust that God could transform it into something beautiful. Amid this self-examination, I found that God's grace was indeed sufficient and that it was greater than my flaws and weaknesses. I learned that true healing begins with self-awareness and humility, acknowledging our need for God's transformative love and mercy. While complicated, this process of self-discovery became a vital step in my journey of faith and healing. It was an opportunity to confront my own humanity and surrender it to the One who could make me whole again and give me beauty for ashes.

Samson, a figure from the Old Testament, is often remembered for his extraordinary physical strength, but his story is far more complex than mere physical prowess. Like me, Samson endeavored with inner battles and vulnerabilities that he had to confront. Samson's story revealed to me that strength, even of the extraordinary kind, does not exempt us from human frailty. Despite his physical might, Samson struggled with personal weaknesses, including issues of trust, impulsivity, and a failure to heed the wisdom of those who cared about him. These vulnerabilities led him into situations of great danger and pain. As I read about Samson's journey, I began to see parallels between his struggles and my own. I recognized the times when I had acted impulsively, ignoring the counsel of loved ones and the wisdom of faith. Samson's story became a mirror through which I could examine my own actions and decisions.

In the aftermath of my divorce, I found myself in a place of brokenness, and it was during this time that I could relate to Samson in unexpected ways. Just as Samson's physical might didn't exempt him from inner battles, my efforts to salvage my marriage had not spared me from the emotional turmoil and spiritual questioning that followed. During this challenging period, I withdrew from my usual support networks just as Samson often acted impulsively and independently. I needed time and space to wrestle with the complexities of my situation, to hear from God, and to make sense of my pain. It felt like I was in a solitary season of self-reflection, much like Samson's moments of isolation.

In the solitude of my struggle, I confronted my own limitations and the realities of life—that sometimes, despite our best efforts, things simply do not work out as we hope. My faith was tested, and I questioned why my prayers seemed to go unanswered. I reached a point where I stopped attending church, not because I lost trust in God but because I could not bear hearing well-meaning advice about trust and prayer when it felt like my world was falling apart. However, as I journeyed through this difficult chapter, I began to glean invaluable insights about myself. I recognized that, like Samson, I had been so consumed by trying to fix my marriage that I had lost sight of my own needs and desires. I was so self-assured by my physical strength that I allowed it to become my weakness. My marriage unraveled, but during this unexpected, I discovered a reservoir of resilience within myself that I had not known existed.

Like Samson, who ultimately found his strength in surrendering to God, I found my own strength through surrendering my pain and confusion. Even when it felt like my prayers went unanswered, I never stopped being faithful or prayerful. In that steadfastness, I emerged from this challenging season stronger and more resilient than ever before. Samson was an Israelite who was chosen by God to be a Nazirite, which meant that he was set apart for a special purpose and had certain rules to follow, including never cutting his hair. Samson was known for his incredible strength, which he believed came from God.

One day, Samson saw a Philistine woman and fell in love with her. He asked his parents to arrange their marriage, but they objected because the Philistines were enemies of Israel. However, Samson insisted on marrying her, and so they wed. At the wedding feast, Samson posed a riddle to some Philistine guests. If they could solve it, he would give them thirty linen garments, but if they could not, they would have to give him thirty linen garments. The Philistines were unable to solve the riddle, so they threatened Samson's wife until she persuaded him to tell her the answer. Samson was angry when he found out, and he left his wife and went back to his parents' home. Later, Samson returned to the Philistines and killed thirty men in revenge for their cheating him in the riddle. This sparked a long feud between Samson and the Philistines.

Samson's strength continued to amaze everyone. Once, he killed a lion with his bare hands, and another time, he killed a thousand Philistines with the jawbone of a donkey. Eventually, Samson fell in love with another Philistine woman named Delilah. The Philistine leaders offered her a large sum of money to find out the secret of Samson's strength. After much persuasion, Samson finally told her that his strength came from his uncut hair. While he was sleeping, Delilah cut off his hair, and he lost his strength. The Philistines captured him and gouged out his eyes. In the end, Samson's hair began to grow back, and he prayed to God for strength one last time. He pushed apart the pillars of the temple where the Philistines were gathered, causing the entire building to collapse and killing himself and thousands of Philistines.

As his strength grew, so did his confidence, and he began to believe that he could handle the casualties of his own weakness. It is a paradoxical aspect of human psychology—we often become overconfident in our areas of strength to the point where we believe we are impervious to the consequences of our weaknesses. Samson, in his remarkable physical prowess, may have felt invincible. This overconfidence led him to make reckless choices, such as revealing the source of his strength to

Delilah, despite the risks involved. Samson's story serves as a cautionary message about the dangers of unchecked self-assurance. His belief in his own abilities blinded him to the very real vulnerabilities that existed in his life. Just as he thought he could handle the casualties of his weaknesses, we, too, can fall into the trap of underestimating the impact of our own vulnerabilities when we become too self-assured.

Much like Samson, I, too, found myself ensnared by a similar illusion. The passing of my son had fortified me with a strength I never knew I had. I felt like I could endure anything that life threw my way. My resolve was unbreakable, and I was determined to press on with determination. However, in the midst of this newfound strength, I neglected to recognize the fragility of my heart. I had been so focused on the power I had gained from my experiences that I did not protect my very core-my heart. Proverbs 4:23 warns us to guard our hearts diligently, for everything we do flows from it.

It is a lesson I had overlooked in my quest for resilience. Just as Samson did not fully grasp the extent of his vulnerability until it was too late, I, too, did not realize the depth of my own fragility until my heart was tested in unexpected ways. It was a humbling realization that strength alone could not shield me from the emotional toll of life's challenges. Recognizing my own weakness became a crucial step in my journey of healing and self-discovery. I learned that true strength is not solely measured by our ability to endure hardships but also by our ability to acknowledge our vulnerabilities and seek support in our faith and relationships.

Like Samson, my story serves as a reminder that even in our moments of strength, we must remain vigilant in guarding our hearts, for it is the wellspring of our lives, and it is in acknowledging our fragility that we find the true source of resilience. Judges 16:25-30 15 says, "And it came to pass, when their hearts were merry, that they said, call for Samson, that he may make us sport. And they called for Samson out of the prison house, and he made them sport: and they set him between the pillars. 26. And Samson said unto the lad that held him by the hand, suffer me that I may feel the pillars whereupon the house standeth, that I may lean upon them. 27. Now the house was full of men and women, and all the lords of the Philistines were there; and there were upon the roof about three thousand men and women, that beheld while Samson made sport.

28. And Samson called unto the Lord, and said, O Lord God, remember me, I pray thee, and strengthen me, I pray thee,

only this once, O God, that I may be at once avenged of the Philistines for my two eyes. 29. And Samson took hold of the two middle pillars upon which the house stood, and on which it was borne up, of the one with his right hand, and of the other with his left. 30. And Samson said, let me die with the Philistines. And he bowed himself with all his might, and the house fell upon the lords, and upon all the people that were therein. So, the dead which he slew at his death were more than they which he slew in his life."

At times, we may find it more convenient to fixate on the ill-treatment we endure at the hands of others rather than taking responsibility for our own choices that led us into those circumstances, making us vulnerable to mistreatment. When it felt like life was tearing me apart, and the consequences of my decisions left me in a place where it seemed defeated, I held onto a powerful truth—a truth I had learned from the story of Samson. Just as Samson's strength returned, even after the depths of his fall, I believed that my own strength could be renewed. I found myself echoing Samson's cry to the Lord, "Remember me, O Lord God." It was a plea that went beyond my circumstances; it was a declaration of my identity as God's servant. I asked God to remember the times when I had carried His joy and when I had felt anointed by His presence.

In this process, I realized that I did not have to experience a physical death to find renewal. Instead, I needed to allow my old self, my weaknesses, and my past mistakes to die. I had to surrender them to God, trusting in His power to bring about transformation and restoration. Just as Samson's hair grew back, symbolizing his return to strength, I, too, experienced a resurgence of purpose, hope, and resilience. It was not my own might but the grace and redemption of God that brought me back from the brink of defeat. In that renewal, I found the strength to carry on with a heart fully surrendered to the One who remembers and restores His servants.

When we go through a difficult time, whether it is a divorce, a loss, or something else entirely, we must remember that we are not alone. Even when it feels like no one can possibly understand what we are going through, there is comfort and strength to be found in our faith. We must trust in God's plan and know that even when things do not make sense, He still walks with us every step we take. "But He said to me, 'My grace is sufficient for you, for my power is made perfect in weakness.' Therefore, I will boast all the more gladly about my weaknesses so that Christ's power may rest on me. That is why, for Christ's sake, I delight in weaknesses, in insults, in hardships, in persecutions, in difficulties.

For when I am weak, then I am strong." Just as 2 Corinthians 12:9-10 reminds us that God's power is made perfect in weakness, we see this truth exemplified in Samson's life. Despite his physical might, Samson's true strength came not from his muscles but from his faith in God. It was in his moments of weakness, such as when he was captured by the Philistines and lost his physical strength, that he turned to God in prayer. Like many of us, Samson had his moments of weakness and vulnerability. However, it was precisely in those moments that God's strength became most evident. Samson's story also offered a message of hope. Despite his shortcomings, God continued to work through Samson to fulfill His purposes.

Dawna Lindsey

ECHOES OF FEAR

Unable to find the words to express it, I found myself drenched in fear, drowning in grief, sinking in sadness, covered in doubt. My emotions were overwhelming; my thoughts were scattered, and I was feeling emotions I did not understand. A battle waged within me. It felt like I was addicted to those emotions.

I was searching for a place where I could honor the Lord with my emotions. A place where I could feel my feelings without being taken over by them. A place where I learn not to lean solely on emotions, which are as tumultuous and unpredictable as the sea, but to lean on the One who controls all winds and waves. A place where I can rejoice in my sufferings, knowing that suffering produces endurance, and endurance produces character, and character produces hope. I needed that hope! A place where I could be still and know that He is God. A place where the suffering itself unexpectedly becomes His answer to that prayer. A place where He would not demand that I suppress or deny my feelings. A place where He would allow me to process them as He sits beside me, right here in the midst of it all, In my tears, confusion, frustration, anger, disappointment, and questioning. In this place, I would know Him as I had never known Him before, His nature as the God of my emotions, the One who fashioned me with care.

For the longest time, my faith in God felt like a rock-solid foundation in most areas of my life. I could trust Him with my hopes, dreams, and struggles, trusting that He had a plan for me, but there was one area where my faith wavered, where I found it excruciatingly difficult to fully surrender - my children. The fear of losing another child weighed like a heavy stone in my heart. Having faced loss in the past, I could not help but carry that burden with me. It was as if the scars from that experience had etched a sense of vulnerability deep within me, and that vulnerability manifested as an abstruse fear for the well-being of my children. I knew in my heart that God was capable of caring for them, just as He cared for me in my darkest moments.

I understood intellectually that His love was boundless, and His plan was perfect, yet when it came to my kids, my emotions ran rampant. I grappled with anxiety and doubt, struggling to fully trust that His divine protection extended to them. It was in these moments of vulnerability that my relationship with God deepened. I began to realize that true faith was not just about trusting Him with the aspects of life that felt secure but also with the areas that terrified me the most.

Embarking on a therapeutic journey, I found a safe haven where I could unburden my soul. For the first time, I felt the relief of sharing my innermost fears and dreams with a living, empathetic listener rather than confining them to the silent pages of my notebooks. I came to understand that vulnerability is not a sign of weakness but a pathway to great transformation. Day by day, I bared my soul to this woman. Yet, life is often unpredictable. One day, as the world suffered from Covid, I eagerly logged into our Zoom session only to be met with unexpected news. My therapist told me that our time together had come to an end; she had accepted a new job opportunity. The weight of her words hit me hard. It felt as if I was being abandoned all over again, triggering the deep-seated issues I had been trying to heal from. The memories of past betrayals and rejections consumed me, and I felt myself spiraling back into a whirlpool of despair and anger. Tears flowed freely, reminiscent of a child's cry for help.

It was a deep desire to heal that had led me to therapy, especially as I wrestled with the shadows of abandonment. However, in my darkest moments, I was gently reminded of a higher power. A power that never wavers never leaves, and is steadfast in its love. God, in his infinite wisdom, nudged me back towards an old coping mechanism – writing. Reconnecting with my pen and paper, I began to channel my emotions into words. The act of writing became therapeutic, allowing me to articulate my pain, hopes, and dreams in a way I could not always verbalize. Through this cathartic process, I rediscovered the strength that lay within, having learned once again to navigate the complexities of my heart and mind.

While therapy was undoubtedly helpful, the most significant insight I gained about myself was that I have a strong inclination toward wanting control in my life. The realization that I lean towards being a 'control enthusiast' has been both enlightening and emotionally overwhelming. It is clear now that this fear of losing control has a negative impact on my emotions, and it is something I have to be intentionally committed to working on in my journey towards healing. While I was going through various experiences, I realized that God was continuously revealing Himself and breaking up the fallow grounds of my heart. Each situation became an opportunity for God to work in my life, tilling the soil of my heart to bring about growth and transformation.

A phone call from my daughter, her voice trembling with tears and anguish, abruptly interrupted my world. She was going through a battle within her own mind, her own storm of self-doubt and torment, one no parent ever wants to witness in their child. Without a moment's hesitation, I rushed home, my heart pounding with concern and a deep desire to comfort her. As I entered her room, I found her in distress, lost in the sea of her thoughts. We sat together, and I instinctively began to pray with her, asking for peace and comfort to envelop her troubled mind. In the midst of that heartfelt prayer, a powerful realization struck me like a bolt of lightning: I am not her god. In that moment, it became profoundly clear that despite my deepest desires to protect and shield my daughter from life's hardships, there were battles they faced that I could not fight for them.

It was a humbling revelation, one that exposed my own lack of power as a parent. As much as I longed to be her protector and guardian, I could not shield my daughter from her own self-sabotaging thoughts or inner struggles. It was a stark reminder that there are aspects of her life, her mind, and her journey that only God could truly understand and navigate. In that moment of repentance and surrender, I relinquished the illusion of control and recognized that my trust in God needed to extend beyond my own life to the lives of my precious children. It was a realization that, in my role as a parent, my most powerful act of love was not trying to be their god but rather pointing them toward the One who could offer them the peace, strength, and guidance they needed in their darkest moments.

As I was driving one night, an unexpected wave of emotions overcame me. Tears began to stream down my face, and at that moment, I felt an urgent need to call on God. With a heavy heart, I pleaded for peace, that elusive sense of calm and serenity that had often seemed just out of reach. As I poured out my heart, an unexpected response seemed to echo within me, as if God Himself were speaking directly to my soul. He gently whispered, "Peace comes with a price." Those words hung in the air. There was a moment of divine revelation, a reminder that peace, the kind that transcends understanding, is not a gift that comes easily. It is not found in the absence of turmoil or adversity, but rather, it is born out of a deeper understanding of life's complexities.

In the midst of these emotions and the inspiring message about the cost of peace, my dreams also carried significant meaning, particularly one recurring dream that intensified my already overwhelming fear of water. In the dream, I found myself on a beautiful island, walking with a lantern in hand, admiring the island and all of its beauty. The night was dark, and the lantern was the only source of light. Suddenly, a huge wave came out of nowhere and pulled me into the water. My lantern went out, and I felt myself drowning. I struggled to stay afloat and could not call for help because I was all alone. I would wake up gasping for air. The dream felt so real. I had the same dream every night for a week. I was terrified and did not know how to make it stop. Then, one night, I decided to turn to God for help.

I prayed and said, "God, I'm scared, but I'm tired of being afraid. If I'm going to have this dream again, I need you to show up and rescue me. And He did. On the last night of this recurring dream, something changed. When the wave pulled me under, God reached out and grabbed my hand. He pulled me out of the water and walked with me through the darkness. I felt safe and protected. The next morning, I woke up with tears in my eyes, but this time they were tears of joy. That dream was a turning point for me. I was reminded again that even in the darkest moments, God is with me, and He can rescue me from my fears.

I was going through a cleansing cycle, a purging season. Psalm 56:8: "You keep track of all my sorrows. You have collected all my tears in your bottle. You have recorded each one in your book." In this verse, the psalmist is speaking to God, acknowledging that God is fully aware of his suffering and emotional distress. The metaphor used is powerful, "You keep track of all my sorrows. You have collected all my tears in your bottle. You have recorded each one in your book." "You keep track of all my sorrows." suggests that God is intimately aware of every hardship, sadness, and difficulty that the psalmist experiences in life.

Nothing goes unnoticed by Him. "You have collected all my tears in your bottle."This metaphor paints a vivid image of God collecting the tears shed by the psalmist as if they were precious and valuable. It symbolizes God's deep concern and empathy for our pain as if He carefully treasures and remembers each tear. "You have recorded each one in your book." This line underscores God's meticulous attention to detail. It implies that God keeps a record of our sorrows and tears, signifying that He remembers our struggles and is always present to comfort and support us. He is intimately aware of our pain, treasures our tears, and keeps a record of our sorrows, showing His loving and caring nature.

In Matthew Chapter 4, After Jesus fed a large crowd with five loaves of bread and two fish, He instructed His disciples to get into a boat and go ahead of Him to the other side of the Sea of Galilee (also known as Lake Tiberias). Jesus then dismissed the crowd and went up into the hills alone to pray. Meanwhile, the disciples were on the boat in the middle of the sea when a strong wind began to blow, and the waves grew rough. They were struggling to make progress when, in the early hours of the morning, they saw Jesus walking on the water toward them. Thinking it was a ghost, they were terrified.

Jesus immediately reassured them, saying, "Take courage! It is I. Don't be afraid." Peter, filled with a mixture of faith and doubt, called out to Jesus, "Lord if it's you, tell me to come to you on the water." Jesus replied, "Come." Peter got out of the boat and started walking on the water toward Jesus. However, as he noticed the strong wind, he became afraid and began to sink.

He cried out, "Lord, save me!" Jesus immediately reached out His hand and caught Peter, saying, "You of little faith, why did you doubt?" As they got back into the boat, the wind ceased, and the disciples worshiped Jesus, declaring, "Truly, you are the Son of God."

This story illustrates the importance of faith and trust in Jesus. While Peter initially had faith by stepping out of the boat, his doubt caused him to falter. Nevertheless, Jesus was there to rescue him, emphasizing the significance of keeping one's eyes on Him in times of fear and uncertainty. Fear has had a tremendous impact on my life, just like the intense winds and turbulent waters that Peter faced when he stepped out of the boat to walk on the water towards Jesus. Peter initially had faith and took that courageous step, but his doubt crept in when he noticed the uncontrollable elements around him.

In the same way, when faced with uncertainty or situations beyond my control, I find myself in a state of anxiety and fear. Just as Peter cried out, "Lord, save me!" When he began to sink, I, too, yearned for help when I felt overwhelmed by circumstances. In his moment of doubt, Jesus was immediately there to save Peter, gently admonishing him for his "little faith." It reminds me that, despite my fear of losing control, there is a higher power, a source of strength and comfort, ready to support me when in need.

God's response to my dream became an echo on my journey, a reminder that peace is worth pursuing, even when it feels distant and costly. It is a reminder that, like a precious gem, peace shines brightest when it has been through the refining process. As I continued to navigate the twists and turns of life, those whispered words served as a beacon of hope, inspiring me to seek the enduring peace that transcends circumstances and offers relief to the weary heart. In order to have peace, I had to trust God, even when trusting God meant stepping out of my comfort zone.

It was a mixture of fear and comfort that kept me anchored in Patterson, Louisiana, my hometown, where I had been my entire life without any desire to change that. Reflecting on the island in my dream, I now see it as a symbol from God, a message that He desired to grant me a life filled with beauty and purpose. However, I realized that I had been letting the waves of life's circumstances pull me under, dimming the light that was meant to shine brightly within me. This realization struck me deeply, fueling my conviction to break free from the shackles of fear and comfort. This conviction led me to make a decision that would reshape my life's trajectory.

With a heart full of faith and a mindset on the pursuit of peace, I packed our things and moved to Texas. This was a leap into the unknown. The decision was daunting, yet I knew it was necessary. To fully rely on God and embrace the beautiful life He had in store for me, stepping out in faith was not just an option but a necessity. Even if it meant leaving behind everything familiar, I was prepared to trust in His plan and follow where He led.

In Acts Chapter 9, there is a story of A man named Ananias who lived in the city of Damascus, during the early days of Christianity. He was a faithful follower of Jesus. At the same time, a zealous persecutor of Christians named Saul of Tarsus was on a mission to arrest and persecute believers in the region. One day, as Saul was traveling to Damascus with his heart full of hostility towards the Christian faith, he encountered a blinding light from heaven. In this radiant light, he heard the voice of Jesus, who asked him why he was persecuting Him. Stricken with blindness, Saul was led into the city by his companions. Meanwhile, Ananias had a vision in which the Lord spoke to him, instructing him to go to a specific house on Straight Street in

Damascus. There, he was to find a man named Saul and lay hands on him so that Saul might regain his sight. Ananias knew of Saul's reputation as a persecutor of Christians, and he hesitated at first, expressing his concerns to the Lord.

Acts 9:10-12 10."In Damascus, there was a disciple named Ananias. The Lord called to him in a vision, 'Ananias!' 'Yes, Lord,' he answered. 11. The Lord told him, 'Go to the house of Judas on Straight Street and ask for a man from Tarsus named Saul, for he is praying. 12. In a vision, he has seen a man named Ananias come and place his hands on him to restore his sight.'"

God assured Ananias that He had a specific purpose for Saul. Ananias obediently went to the house as instructed. Finding Saul in a state of blindness and confusion, he placed his hands upon him, and miraculously, Saul's sight was restored. Moreover, Ananias baptized Saul, marking his conversion to Christianity. Through this extraordinary encounter, Saul's heart was transformed, and he became known as the apostle Paul, a fervent preacher of the gospel and one of the most influential figures in the early Christian church. Ananias's obedience, despite his initial fears, played a pivotal role in this remarkable conversion, highlighting the transformative power of faith and God's ability to change the hearts of even the most passionate adversaries of the Christian faith.

Just as Saul journeyed into the city of Damascus, blind and uncertain, I felt a similar sense of being led into the unknown when I moved to Texas. Saul's experience on the road to Damascus was a pivotal moment of transformation, where he, once blinded, was led into a city he did not know. In my life, this echoed through my dream, which I believe was a divine guide leading me towards a new path, much like Saul being led by the hand into Damascus.

Upon his arrival, Saul encountered Ananias, a man chosen by God to play a crucial role in his transformation. Similarly, in Texas, I encountered individuals who were, I believe, placed in my life by God. These encounters were not by chance but were divinely orchestrated, much like Ananias was for Saul. Just as Saul's encounter led to a substantial change, from his name to his vision and, ultimately, his purpose, my encounters in Texas brought about significant changes in my life. These people helped restore my vision in a spiritual sense and aided in the transformation of my understanding of God's purpose for me.

This parallel with Saul's story highlights a fundamental truth: God often sends us into the unknown so that He can do the work of restoring and refocusing us. It is in these unfamiliar territories, away from our comfort zones, that we are compelled to place our trust entirely in Him. In doing so, we allow God to reveal and set our eyes on the purpose He has for us, just as He did for Saul, who emerged from his experience as Paul with a new vision and mission.

In the dream, I felt the overwhelming force of the water. The fear of being swept away and the struggle to keep my head above the surface. It was a reminder of how fear could be like that relentless wave, knocking me off my feet and holding me back. I knew, deep within, that God was trying to communicate something important. He was letting me know that there was a purpose, a plan, something He wanted to do in my life. I needed to trust Him. I had been allowing fear to drown out His intentions. I was unable to see past the turbulent waters that surrounded me. I felt alone in the dream and as if the lantern was my only source of light. It was when I called on Him, placing my hand in His hand and accepting the invitation to trust God, to let go of the fear that had been paralyzing me, that I was able to see that I was holding myself back in the water.

Houston was a place that initially felt intimidating and overwhelming, a city where the unfamiliarity of it all cast a shadow of uncertainty over my life. However, it was precisely during this intimidating environment that God began to unveil a series of "aha" moments, shedding light on why He had placed me there. God was diligently tilling the fallow grounds of my heart. Every day, as I stepped outside, I would hear the joyful symphony of birds chirping in the trees, and inexplicably, tears would stream down my face. Their song seemed to touch something hidden deep inside of me. Similarly, the laughter of children, so carefree and full of innocence, had the power to move me to tears. Their unrestrained joy and genuine laughter acted as a mirror reflecting the emotions I often kept concealed. In those moments, I realized that God was using the simple, everyday sounds of nature and the unbridled laughter of children as tools to break down the barriers I had built around my heart. He was softening my soul, helping me release pent-up emotions, and inviting me to embrace vulnerability.

Ananias, faced with a daunting task, exemplified trust in God's guidance. He bravely overcame his fear to follow God's command, demonstrating great faith and obedience by journeying to Saul, laying his hands upon him, and restoring Saul's sight. Similarly, in the narrative of Peter stepping onto the tempestuous waters, we witness a moment of remarkable faith in response to Jesus' call. As he ventured onto the water towards Jesus, it was a testament to extraordinary faith. However, Peter's faith briefly wavered when he became acutely aware of the fierce winds and crashing waves. Yet, even in the midst of doubt and fear, Peter's immediate cry to Jesus led to an outstretched hand of salvation.

My own journey, marked by a pivotal dream and the courageous decision to move to Texas, echoes the lives of Peter, Saul, and Ananias, where faith, trust, and obedience play central roles in overcoming immense challenges. These stories underscore the paramount importance of faith, trust, and obedience—even in the face of seemingly insurmountable challenges. Much like the divine intervention that guided Peter on the water, transformed Saul through Ananias, and led me to a new life in Texas, these stories collectively reinforce a penetrating truth. When we face our fears with faith and obedience, we invite God's presence and deliverance, turning our challenges into pathways of transformation and renewal.

As I reflected on the striking parallels between my exploration of moving in obedience to God's voice and the experiences of Ananias and Saul, as well as Peter walking on water with Jesus, I found inspiration in their obedience and faith.

It was a compelling invitation to embrace vulnerability and summon courage, fully aware that in doing so, I might unearth the impactful ways in which God could work both within and through me. In the course of time, I received a call. It was an offer to work in the Hawaii Department of Education, a job I had never applied for in a place surrounded by the very fear that had been deeply rooted within me - water.

Hawaii, with its breathtaking landscapes and serene beaches, was a dream destination for many, but for me, it was a land both alluring and daunting due to my fear of water. However, I mentioned wanting to visit while the thought of living on an island, encompassed by the vast, uncharted ocean, stirred a sense of anxiety within me. Yet, there it was—a call, a beckoning from the unknown, a chance to confront my fears head-on. It felt as though God was inviting me to move beyond my comfort zone once again to break free from the constraints I had imposed on myself and to place an even deeper trust in Him than ever before. I was afraid, especially considering that I had made significant life changes to move to Hawaii.

Still, despite my efforts, I met a series of obstacles and challenges that ultimately led me to give up on the opportunity of moving and working in Hawaii. I couldn't see it clearly at the time, and despite thinking I was prepared for travel, I found myself constantly trying to arrange and control every detail. God's plan was for me to travel, but He wanted me to relinquish control and place my trust fully in Him. Unfortunately, I struggled with this surrender.

I had taken my daughter skating. We chose an extremely popular skating rink in Houston where expert skaters showcased their prowess, gliding smoothly across the floor. With each of them zooming past, I tried to teach Justice the basics right at the rink's center. However, as the rush of skaters moved around us, creating drafts of wind as they sped by, one particularly swift gust knocked her balance. Tears welled up in her eyes, and she exclaimed, "Momma, I cannot do it!" I held her firmly, trying to instill confidence, Justice, and trust in me. I am holding you. Just keep moving your feet.

Yet, she was too overwhelmed and paralyzed by fear. It was clear that the skillful skaters around her were intimidating. I told her, Look around. All of these skilled skaters? They started just like you with wobbly feet, countless falls, but relentless spirit. They got up each time they fell, and over time, they mastered it. If you never take that step, you will always remain here, uncertain and afraid. Later, while praying for guidance, I was reminded of that day at the rink.

ECHOES OF THE HEART

Imagine attending family gatherings and being confronted with the gaze of a relative who has caused you deep pain. Each encounter is a piercing reminder of past wounds, reopening them anew. While he seems to be enjoying himself, I am often consumed with thoughts about his character and actions. One day, he touched my daughter's face, and a surge of intense anger welled up within me, an emotion so potent that it evoked the darkest of thoughts. The past and the present tangled, and it was a challenge to contain the tempest of emotions inside.

Life has dealt me its fair share of pain. I have felt the sting of betrayal from those I believed should have been my protectors, from those I deeply cared for and loved. Over time, I poured so much of myself into others that I was left empty, without a semblance of self-care or understanding of how to support my own well-being. This abandonment turned to anger. Part of me wished I could despise those who had wronged me, believing I had every right to harbor such feelings. The very idea of forgiveness seemed insurmountable. Why was it up to me to forgive those who showed no remorse? Those who, after causing me pain, behaved as if I was indebted to them? Those who gave no indication that they wouldn't repeat their hurtful actions? The weight of my bitterness grew heavy. Yet, as time went on, I realized that by clinging to this bitterness and withholding forgiveness, I was inflicting more pain upon myself than upon those who had wronged me.

As I highlighted, God had started a deep work within me, tilling my heart to break up its fallow grounds. I plunged myself into activities: I intensified my workouts, took up gardening, and immersed myself in various tasks. I yearned to keep my mind preoccupied, for haunting thoughts began to resurface— thoughts so daunting that, at times, I locked myself in the bathroom to prevent them from materializing into actions. I had to focus my ears only on music that glorified God.

These were thoughts I had to sing and worship over, thoughts I felt too mortified to share—violent, lustful, paranoid, and psychotic musings far from the mind of Christ. I deeply yearned for God to intervene, to overhaul my thought patterns, to extricate me from my former self, and to mold me into His intended design. It felt like an endless loop—periods of calm, then tumult. I desperately sought healing, deliverance, and true transformation from the inside out.

While the world outside grappled with the COVID-19 pandemic, my vocals began to falter, and it took months before I could see a doctor. Fear gripped me, leading me to find comfort in alcohol. I prayed, yet I simultaneously turned to drinking. My faith waned, even though I knew better. A pressing self-reflection arose: Did my self-perception mirror Christ's nature and mindset? Was each life experience molding me closer to Christ's very likeness? The answer was a resounding NO. The reflection in the mirror displeased me—it wasn't just my external image but my thoughts about myself. I perceived a prominent presence of "SELF": self-loathing, self-pity, self-righteousness, and a selfish attitude toward God.

On paper, I ticked the boxes of a devout Christian. I acknowledged and believed in Jesus, the risen Son of God. I was baptized, regularly read the Bible, prayed, attended church, gave tithes, and spread God's word. I practiced kindness even when it wasn't convenient. Yet, upon introspection, I recognized areas that starkly contrasted the character of Christ. For my birthday, we were still quarantined, so my sister contacted all my closest friends and organized a surprise party online. During the party, my sister asked my friends to start off by sharing their most memorable moments with me. Each one of them mentioned ways I inspired them. My cousin said, "I remember her first time preaching, how well she had done, and how much she inspired me. I was proud of her and how she had grown in Christ and was walking in her calling." A couple of my friends had mentioned how "strong I was and how I'm always encouraging them with the word of God." That video call was more meaningful than they could imagine! The Holy Spirit convicted me! Sometimes, we forget our identity in Christ. It was so easy for me to speak the word to others, but I was not living by the word.

I found myself pleading with God to silence not just the external doubters but also the skeptical voice within me. The irony was not lost on me – how could I offer joy and hope to others through God's word yet harbor doubts about Him extending the same grace to me? My faith was intact, but I battled with feelings of unworthiness and struggled to accept the vastness of God's forgiveness. The distractions around us and the fleeting desires of our minds should not be our guiding light. Instead, our souls' true necessities should lead us. By earnestly seeking God, we position ourselves to be recipients of His abundant blessings. I confess there have been numerous occasions where my emotions clouded my judgment, leading to actions that didn't reflect a Christ-like nature.

At times, the seeds of doubt in our hearts are sown by our own hesitations. We might not always lay out our entire selves before God, holding back certain aspects due to shame, neglect, or fear of vulnerability. While we might momentarily forget or suppress these hidden facets, they don't forget us and continue to weigh on our souls. These can range from deeply buried memories to covert desires and concealed secrets. It is essential that we earnestly seek God's illumination on these shadowy corners of our hearts. By doing so, we invite true liberation from the shackles with which these secrets bind us. Only when these concealed truths are brought to light can we truly soften our hearts and avoid spiritual imprisonment.

I confess that I am often quick to be irritated by seemingly minor inconveniences. Once, I stood in a store line, growing increasingly impatient with a cashier I perceived as too slow. In my mind, all I saw was an inconvenient five-minute delay, failing to consider that perhaps she was enduring a tough day or facing her own personal challenges. Instead of recognizing a fellow human in need of understanding, I inadvertently became one ruder customer she had to handle that day. Reflecting on the boundless grace God bestows upon us should make it easier for us to extend that same grace to others. That seems so small, but it was small little moments that needed to be plucked up and rooted out of my heart. Psalm 4:23 says, "Keep thy heart with all diligence; for out of it are the issues of life."

When memories of my son flood back, tears would blur my vision. In those heart-wrenching instances, anger towards God would consume me, a burning question of "Why?" echoing in my mind. Yet, in the midst of my anguish, a scripture often surfaces, guiding me towards peace: "Create in me a clean heart, O God, and renew a steadfast spirit within me" (Psalm 51:10). This psalm was a plea for forgiveness and purification by King David after his transgression with Bathsheba that caused the death of their son.

At times, this verse becomes my sole prayer, a fervent plea, for amidst my pain and confusion, my deepest yearning is still unchanged - to love and serve God with an undivided heart. For that, I recognize the need for untainted hands and a heart untarnished by bitterness. Psalm 24:3-4, "Who shall ascend into the hill of the LORD? or who shall stand in his holy place? He that hath clean hands, and a pure heart; who hath not lifted up his soul unto vanity, nor sworn deceitfully." This psalm speaks of those who are worthy to worship the Lord and stand in His holy presence, emphasizing purity of actions ("clean hands") and intentions ("pure heart").

Finding the strength to forgive is one of life's most challenging tasks. Yet, the wellspring from which I draw this strength is the unparalleled forgiveness Jesus bestows upon me. It becomes imperative to recall that the gift of grace, so freely given to us, is meant for all, including those who have hurt us. At times, the temptation to be self-serving looms large, making it seem like an easier option than extending grace. Colossians 3:13 offers insightful wisdom on this matter, stating, "Bear with each other and forgive one another if any of you has a grievance against someone. Forgive as the Lord forgave you."

God's unconditional love for us is often expressed through His act of forgiveness. And He wishes for us to reflect that love by forgiving others in our lives. When we do, it acts as a testament to His boundless grace, guiding others towards Him. The imperative to forgive is underscored by three pivotal reasons: firstly, because God continuously forgives our transgressions; secondly, because holding onto bitterness and resentment only poisons our own soul; and thirdly, because we cannot genuinely receive the blessings of forgiveness if we are not ready to offer the same to others.

In 1 Corinthians 9:24, we are reminded, "Do you not know that in a race, all runners run, but only one receives the prize? So run that you may obtain it." Consider the world of track and field. Athletes navigate through hurdles, engage in high jumps, participate in relays, and sprint towards the finish line. Amongst the cheers and the tension in the air, they prepare themselves at the starting line, heads held high and chests puffed out, their eyes fixed on the ultimate prize. A racer's primary aim is to shed anything that could diminish his speed or focus.

I recall when my son was competing in track meets. Before his races, he would entrust me with his additional clothing, shoes, cell phone, and any other belongings. He was not preoccupied with his possessions; his singular focus was the race ahead. He knew they were taken care of, allowing them to run unencumbered. Similarly, in our life's race, we must lay down our anxieties, pain, apprehensions, and any weight that slows us down, entrusting them to our Heavenly Father and running forward with steadfast focus.

Reflecting on track and field rules offers further spiritual insights. Transparent Clothing Rule: Athletes' apparel must remain opaque even when wet and should not distract officials. This brings to mind 1 Corinthians 8:9, which advises us against becoming stumbling blocks for others. Relay Baton Exchanges: Athletes in relay races must seamlessly pass batons. This echoes Matthew 28:19-20, where we are commanded to propagate God's message, assured of His continual presence. Staying in the Assigned Lane: Just as athletes are required to remain in their designated lanes, we too, must stay true to our divine path, avoiding deviations.

Dawna Lindsey

ECHOES OF SURRENDER

Discipleship refers to the process of becoming a follower of Jesus Christ and committing oneself to both His teachings and the embodiment of those teachings in one's life. It involves not only learning but also living out that learning in practical, daily actions. Here are some aspects that give a fuller picture of biblical discipleship:

Following Jesus: The most fundamental aspect of discipleship is following Jesus. In the Gospels, Jesus often called out to people, saying, "Follow me." This was an invitation to a relationship and a commitment to adopt His ways, His values, and His mission. Matthew 9:9-13 "As Jesus passed on from there, He saw a man called Matthew sitting at the tax booth, and He said to him, 'Follow me.' And he rose and followed Him. And as Jesus had dinner at the table in the house, behold, many tax collectors and sinners came and ate with Jesus and His disciples. And when the Pharisees saw this, they said to His disciples, 'Why does your teacher eat with tax collectors and sinners?' But when He heard it, He said, 'Those who are well have no need of a physician, but those who are sick. Go and learn what this means: 'I desire mercy and not sacrifice.' For I came not to call the righteous, but sinners."

Upon hearing Jesus's call, Matthew immediately left his job as a tax collector—a position that was often looked down upon in Jewish society for its associations with the Roman occupation and perceived dishonesty. His immediate response underscores the powerful draw of Jesus's invitation. After Matthew starts following Jesus, they dine together, and many other tax collectors join them. This scene signifies the inclusiveness of Jesus's ministry; he reached out to those marginalized or ostracized in society. The Pharisees were critical of Jesus for associating with "sinners." However, Jesus's response—that He came not for the righteous but for the sinners—highlights the core of His mission. His reference to desiring "mercy, and not sacrifice" underscores that the heart's condition and genuine repentance matter more than mere ritualistic practices.

Transformation: True discipleship involves a transformative journey. It is not just about external adherence to rituals or traditions but an inner transformation. As Paul writes in Romans 12:2, "Do not be conformed to this world but be transformed by the renewal of your mind." Before Transformation, Impulsive and Fearful, Peter was among the first disciples called by Jesus. He was known for his strong faith but also for his impulsiveness. For instance, he was the one who stepped out of the boat to walk on water towards Jesus but began sinking due to doubt (Matthew 14:28-31). Peter also declared he would never deny Jesus, yet he denied Him three times on the night of Jesus' arrest out of fear (Matthew 26:69-75).

The Transformative Moment, Post-Resurrection Encounter, After Jesus' resurrection, He appeared to the disciples by the Sea of Tiberias. Here, Jesus had a significant conversation with Peter. He asked Peter three times if he loved Him, mirroring the three times Peter denied Him. Each time, Peter affirmed his love, and Jesus instructed him, "Feed my lambs... Tend my sheep... Feed my sheep" (John 21:15-17). This was not only a restoration of Peter but a commission for his future leadership role in the church.

After Transformation, a Bold Proclaimer and Church Leader, Post-Pentecost, filled with the Holy Spirit, Peter transformed from a man who denied Jesus out of fear to a bold proclaimer of the gospel. His sermon in Acts 2 led to about three thousand people being baptized. He took on a leadership role in the early church, faced persecution without backing down, and played a pivotal role in the inclusion of Gentiles into the Christian community. Peter's transformation story showcases how one can move from doubt, fear, and impulsiveness to a steadfast, bold, and Spirit-led life. Jesus' forgiveness, guidance, and the empowerment of the Holy Spirit led Peter to mature in his faith and become a foundational figure in the growth of the early church.

Teaching and Learning: Discipleship involves deep engagement with the teachings of Jesus. In the Great Commission (Matthew 28:18-20), Jesus tells His disciples to "go and make disciples of all nations, baptizing them... and teaching them to obey everything I have commanded you." Timothy was introduced to us in the New Testament as a believer who was well spoken of by the brethren (Acts 16:1-2). His mother was a

Jewish believer, and his father was Greek. Paul often referred to Timothy as his "son in the faith" (1 Timothy 1:2). This indicates a deep relationship where Paul played the role of a spiritual mentor and guide. Paul not only preached alongside Timothy but also invested time in teaching him essential doctrines and practices. We see evidence of this in the two pastoral epistles, 1 Timothy and 2 Timothy, where Paul gives instructions, warnings, and encouragement.

In 2 Timothy 2:2, Paul says: "And the things you have heard me say in the presence of many witnesses entrust to reliable people who will also be qualified to teach others." Here, Paul emphasizes the importance of teaching and the passing on of foundational Christian truths from one believer to another. Following Paul's teachings and guidance, Timothy became a key leader in the early church, specifically in Ephesus. He faced challenges, including false teachings, which Paul equipped him to handle through his letters. The relationship between Paul and Timothy is a practical example of the Great Commission. Paul evangelized, baptized, and then ensured Timothy was taught all that Christ commanded. Timothy, in turn, was expected (and equipped) to do the same for others.

Commitment and Cost: Discipleship is not a casual endeavor. It demands dedication and often involves sacrifices. Jesus emphasized this when He said, "Whoever wants to be my disciple must deny themselves and take up their cross daily and follow me" (Luke 9:23). I identify with the disciples in their journey of faith. Like them, I have had to deny myself, take up my cross, and follow Jesus. This has involved giving up personal desires in order to prioritize serving God and others, facing challenges and hardships in order to remain faithful to Jesus, and seeking to follow His example in every aspect of my life. While it can be difficult at times, I am reminded of the great rewards that come with following Jesus - a deep sense of purpose and joy, a meaningful community of fellow believers, and the assurance of eternal life with Christ.

We have to Carry Our Cross. This means resonating deeply with Christ's teachings and sacrifices. There are many times I have treated Jesus just as His disciples had. No matter how much I know about Him, no matter how much I walk with Him, no matter how many miracles I have seen with my own eyes, no matter how much time I have spent with Him, there are moments I still doubt and deny Him, not in words but in action. No matter how much I have denied and doubted Him, He still faced persecution for me. "Greater love has no one than this: to lay down one's life for one's friends." John 15:13.

Being willing to face persecution, hardships, and challenges in order to follow Jesus can be a difficult concept to understand. Metaphorical examples include standing up for one's beliefs even when it is unpopular, sacrificing personal time and resources to serve others, and overcoming personal struggles and weaknesses in order to grow in faith. Taking up one's cross is important because it demonstrates our commitment to Jesus and our willingness to follow Him no matter what. There will be times when we will need to intercede on behalf of those who have hurt or betrayed us, showcasing our Christ-like nature by bearing their burdens and presenting them to the Lord's healing touch.

We must Wholeheartedly Follow God. Our journey with God asks us to lay down our individualistic desires, ambitions, emotions, plans, intentions, and ego-driven decisions at the foot of the cross. We are called to pursue Christ's path, even when it challenges our comfort zones, even when we're not in the mood, and even when the way forward appears daunting. Jesus exemplified the epitome of selflessness, always prioritizing the Father's design above His personal desires. The beauty of this surrender lies in the divine promise: by uniting with Christ in death to our old selves, we are assured a place with Him in His resurrection.

Community: While personal commitment and transformation are integral to discipleship, it also has a communal dimension. Disciples are called to be part of a faith community, supporting and being supported by fellow believers. Certainly! The story of Barnabas and the early believers in Jerusalem beautifully illustrates the communal dimension of discipleship. Acts 4:32-37 The passage begins with a description of the early believers: "All the believers were one in heart and mind." This emphasizes that their faith was not just a personal endeavor but was deeply rooted in a community of like-minded individuals. Verse 32 says, "No one claimed that any of their possessions was their own, but they shared everything they had." This radical sharing reflects the depth of their commitment to one another and the communal aspect of their discipleship.

The apostles continued to testify to the resurrection of Jesus with great power, and the text notes that God's grace was powerfully at work within them all. This grace wasn't just working individually but within the entire community. There was no needy person among them. Whenever believers sold land or houses, they brought the money and put it at the apostles' feet to be distributed to anyone who had need. Barnabas (which means "son of encouragement") sold a field he owned, brought the money, and laid it at the apostles' feet. This act of generosity by Barnabas not only contributed to the community's needs but also set a precedent for other believers.

Mission: Being a disciple also means participating in the larger mission of spreading the Gospel and demonstrating God's love through acts of service, compassion, and justice. Let's take a look at Philip and the Ethiopian Eunuch in Acts 8:26-40. Philip, one of the seven chosen to serve in the early church, was directed by an angel of the Lord to go south to the road that descends from Jerusalem to Gaza. His mission was not specified, but he obediently went. On his journey, Philip encountered an Ethiopian eunuch, a high official of the Candace, queen of the Ethiopians. The eunuch was reading from the book of Isaiah, but he did not fully grasp what he was reading.

Seizing the opportunity, Philip approached him and began with that very scripture, explaining the good news about Jesus. The eunuch, upon understanding the message of salvation, expressed his desire to be baptized, and Philip baptized him. After the encounter, the Spirit of the Lord took Philip away, and the eunuch did not see him again but went on his way rejoicing.

Philip, on the other hand, continued preaching the gospel in all the towns from Azotus to Caesarea.

This story showcases multiple facets of discipleship in the context of mission. Obedience to God's Direction as Philip followed God's prompting, even without knowing the exact reason. Proclamation of the Gospel as Philip took the chance to explain the Scriptures and share the message of Jesus, leading to the eunuch's conversion. Acts of Service as Philip didn't just teach; he also performed the act of baptism, welcoming the eunuch into the community of believers. The Ethiopian eunuch, now a believer, would potentially carry the gospel message back to his homeland, further spreading the faith.

Trusting God's Plan: Proverbs 3:5-6 instructs believers to "Trust in the LORD with all your heart and lean not on your own understanding; in all your ways submit to him, and he will make your paths straight." Surrender involves trusting God even when His plans don't align with our understanding.

Giving up Control: The act of surrender involves relinquishing control. I discerned a parallel between my situation and my daughter's initial attempts at skating. I was clinging to God, seeking guidance and direction, yet I was immobilized by my fears and apprehensions. I expected divine intervention without taking any initiative. It dawned on me that just as I encouraged my daughter to move her feet, I, too, had to step forward in faith, trusting God's plan and presence every step of the way. Only by moving could I progress. I had to get out of my own way and allow God to control me. Anything you cannot control is teaching you how to let go.

Repentance and Turning to God: Acts 3:19 says, "Repent, then, and turn to God, so that your sins may be wiped out." Surrendering to God often involves acknowledging one's sins, repenting, and then turning back to God. For example, The Prodigal Son Luke 15:11-32 The younger of two sons asks his father for his share of the inheritance. Once he gets it, he travels to a distant country and squanders it all in reckless living. A severe famine arises in that country, and the son finds himself in need. He takes up a job feeding pigs and is so destitute that he even longs to eat the food the pigs are eating. It is at this moment of deep despair that he reflects upon his actions. The son acknowledges his mistakes, saying to himself, "How many of my father's hired servants have more than enough bread, but I perish here with hunger!"

He decides to return to his father and say, "Father, I have sinned against heaven and before you. I am no longer worthy to be called your son. Treat me as one of your hired servants." He sets off for his father's house. While he is still far off, his father sees him and is filled with compassion, runs to him, embraces him, and kisses him. The son confesses, "Father, I have sinned against heaven and before you. I am no longer worthy to be called your son." But the father orders his servants to bring the best robe, a ring for his finger, and sandals for his feet. He also orders a feast to celebrate the return of his lost son. The father says, "For this, my son was dead and is alive again; he was lost and is found."

A Continuous Act: Surrender is not just a one-time act; it is an ongoing process in a believer's life. It is a continuous commitment to yield to God's authority daily.

ECHOES OF LOVE

The Book of Job is a complex and passional book of the Old Testament that deals with the themes of human suffering, divine justice, and the nature of God's relationship with humanity.

Job 1-2: Job is introduced as a blameless and upright man, wealthy and blessed with a large family. He lives in the land of Uz. In the heavenly courts, Satan challenges Job's piety, suggesting Job is righteous only because he has been blessed. Satan argues that if Job were to lose everything, he would surely curse God. God allows Satan to test Job but forbids him from harming Job physically. Consequently, Job loses his wealth, his children die, and his health deteriorates. Despite his immense suffering, Job does not curse God but struggles to understand why this is happening to him.

Job's Dialogues with His Friends Job 3-31: Job's friends Eliphaz, Bildad, and Zophar come to comfort him. Instead of consolation, they insist that Job must have sinned to deserve such suffering. The friends argue that God is just and only punishes the wicked. Therefore, Job's suffering must be a punishment for some wrongdoing. Job vehemently denies any wrongdoing. He defends his integrity and, in his anguish, wishes for a mediator between himself and God. Elihu enters and expresses anger at Job for justifying himself rather than God and at the three friends for failing to provide an answer to Job's suffering.

God's Response Job 38-41: God finally speaks to Job out of a whirlwind but does not supply direct answers to Job's questions. Instead, God describes the vastness and complexity of the universe, highlighting the mysteries of creation that are beyond human understanding. The point seems to be that humans, with their limited perspective, cannot grasp the entirety of God's plan and purpose.

In conclusion, Job 42: Job acknowledges God's sovereignty and repents for questioning His wisdom. God rebukes Job's friends for their misguided advice and asks Job to pray for them. Job's fortunes are restored, receiving double what he had lost. He is blessed with ten more children and lives for another 140 years. Throughout the story, Job's faith is tested, but he never curses God. The Book of Job emphasizes the importance of trust in God's wisdom and righteousness even when circumstances are beyond human understanding.

Some might wonder how a compassionate and benevolent God could allow Job to undergo such devastating suffering. Yet, it is only through the crucible of adversity that we can truly grasp the depths of the Father's love for His children. Unless we have weathered the storms of life, felt the weight of despair, and yet still experienced the touch of divine love guiding us through the boundless scope of His affection, for we cannot fully fathom the elaborate weaving of God's purpose and the boundless scope of His affection for us. In the echoes of grief, I find a sacred refuge in the enduring wisdom of Job.

Remembering the words of 2 Corinthians 12:9, I embrace the knowledge that God's grace is sufficient for me, and His power is made perfect in my weakness. As I journey through the valleys, I am reminded of Romans 8:17, understanding that in sharing in Christ's sufferings, I am also heir to the glory that will be revealed. In surrendering to God's plan, I discover a strength and enduring grace amidst the ruins of loss. Navigating through the aftermath of great loss often feels like traversing a desolate landscape, and each step is weighed down by the shadows of doubt and despair. As adversities multiplied, my faith trembled, casting uncertainty upon the prospect of a brighter future. Yet, amidst my darkest hours, when all seemed lost, I discovered a constant refuge in God. Despite the wavering of my faith, it remained my sole lifeline.

In suffering, I acknowledge that faith serves as the essence of our hopes and the assurance of unseen realities. "Now faith is the substance of things hoped for, the evidence of things not seen." Hebrews 11:1 encapsulates the essence of faith as a foundational aspect. Faith is the "substance" of things hoped for. This implies that faith gives a tangible reality or essence to our hopes and desires. It is not just wishful thinking or optimism. It provides a firm foundation upon which our hopes are built.

Faith is also described as the "evidence" of things not seen. This suggests that faith provides convincing proof or assurance of realities that are beyond our physical perception. It is about trusting in the truth of God's promises and believing in things that may not yet be visible or tangible in our present circumstances. Faith is not based solely on what we can see or touch but on our confident trust in God and His promises. It is about holding steadfast to our beliefs, even when we cannot see immediate evidence of their fulfillment, knowing that God is faithful and will bring about what He has promised.

When I was compelled to leave my home behind, His grace ensured. I was never truly without shelter. While the pain of losing my son was immeasurable, there is joy in the knowledge that he is in a place of eternal peace, his soul embraced by divine love. In sickness, God became my healing balm, comforting me in my weakest moments and restoring my strength. When I felt like I was on the brink of losing my mind, God's mercy kept me sane. His loving kindness became a stabilizing force that kept me grounded.

The parable of God leaving the ninety-nine to find the one is a well-known parable told by Jesus in the Bible. It is often referred to as the Parable of the Lost Sheep and is found in the Gospels of Matthew (Matthew 18:12-14) and Luke (Luke 15:3-7). This parable is one of several stories in which Jesus illustrates the love and concern that God has for everyone, even those who have strayed or become lost. Once, there was a shepherd who had a flock of one hundred sheep. These sheep were precious to him, and he cared for them with great diligence. He would lead them to green pastures and fresh water, protecting them from harm and danger.

One day, as the shepherd was counting his sheep, he realized that one was missing. Ninety-nine sheep were safely with him, but one had wandered off, lost in the wilderness. The shepherd knew that he could not simply ignore the lost sheep and focus on the rest. He loved each sheep deeply, and the one that was lost weighed heavily on his heart. Leaving the ninety-nine sheep in the safety of the fold, the shepherd embarked on a determined search for the missing one. He scoured the rugged terrain, calling out for the lost sheep, never giving up hope of finding it. His search was relentless, and he was willing to go to great lengths to rescue the one who had gone astray.

After a long search, the shepherd's efforts were rewarded. He found the lost sheep, tired and frightened, trapped in a thicket or a rocky crevice. Without hesitation, the shepherd gently lifted the wayward sheep onto his shoulders, rejoicing that he had found it. Filled with joy, the shepherd returned to his home, calling together his friends and neighbors to celebrate. He shared the good news of the lost sheep being found, and there was great rejoicing. The shepherd's love for the one lost sheep was clear to all, and his care and compassion were a testament to his commitment to each member of his flock. In telling this parable, Jesus conveyed an empathic message about God's love and concern for each individual soul.

Just as the shepherd in the story left the ninety-nine sheep to search for the one that was lost, so too does God show constant love and mercy toward those who have strayed or become lost in life. It is a reminder that no one is beyond the reach of God's grace and that He will go to great lengths to bring back those who have wandered from Him. The Parable of the Lost Sheep serves as a powerful illustration of God's boundless love, His relentless pursuit of the lost, and the joy in heaven when even one soul repents and returns to Him. It teaches us about the value of each individual in God's eyes and the depth of His love and care for His children.

The story of Job and the parable of the lost sheep both reflect the agape love and commitment God has for His children, a love that I have personally witnessed in my own life. When I think of the parable of the lost sheep, I am reminded of times in my life when I felt lost or distant from God. Yet, in those moments of spiritual wandering, I realized that God never left my side.

I was suffocating in depression. Each day felt heavier than the last, and the pain of loss seemed insurmountable. In anguish, I turned to the temporary relief of alcohol, seeking comfort in its numbing embrace. I allowed myself to be consumed by behaviors that I knew were contrary to the path God had set before me. Anger festered within me like a relentless storm, and I directed my wrath towards the very source of my faith. Blinded by bitterness, I convinced myself that my actions were justified, that my rebellion against God was warranted. In my arrogance, I believed I could outrun His love, that my defiance would sever the ties that bound me to Him. Yet, even as I sought to push God away, His love pursued me.

When I attempted to drown out His voice with the clamor of my self-destructive choices, He spoke to me with gentle persistence, calling me back. Though I turned my back on Him, denying the very essence of His existence, His mercy remained steadfast. With each stumble, He extended a hand to lift me from the depths of my despair. When I feigned ignorance of His presence, He showered me with grace beyond measure, refusing to abandon me to the abyss of my own making. Amid my rebellion, God's love proved unyielding. It was a love that refused to be shaken by my doubt or swayed by my anger. It was a love that chased me down when I strayed, pulling me back into the warmth of His embrace. And in the end, it was this relentless love that ultimately led me back to the path of redemption and restoration.

God pursued me, much like the shepherd searches for the lost sheep. Every time I turned back to Him, whether in repentance or seeking comfort, I could feel His joy, like the joy in heaven over one sinner who repents. My journey with God, filled with its mountain and valley moments, is a testament to His limitless love, patience, and commitment. Just as God remained with Job throughout his trials and just as the shepherd went to great lengths to find the one lost sheep, I have felt God's presence in my life, guiding, loving, and restoring me every step of the way.

Dawna Lindsey

THE ECHOES OF A GOOD FATHER

The challenges of life confused me, especially when the opportunity to work in Hawaii had presented itself. Rearranging my life's pieces to fit this new puzzle, only to see it not materialize. Fast forward to the current school year. There, I was on the brink of accepting a position that did not align with my financial expectations. Just as I was about to give in, the phone rang with another offer. While a surge of excitement was the expected reaction, I remained composed. Every time I sought clarity in prayer, the words "Be still and know" resonated in my heart, and I heeded that divine advice, choosing patience over haste. In that stillness, God unveiled plans grander than I could have ever imagined.

I embarked on the journey to Hawaii, and as I sat there on the airplane, waves of reflection washed over me. I was struck by the unexplainable goodness of God that has graced my life. There existed an enormous amount of gratitude within me that defies mere words. Through countless experiences, some perplexing in the moment, I had come to realize the complex design woven by God's hand. His clarity had been a guiding light, and I found myself within a season of "aha" moments again, where revelations from Him consistently brought a smile to my face. The allure of Hawaii was not merely about its breathtaking landscapes; it was a lesson in surrendering and entrusting my burdens to the Almighty. God, in His unique way, brought me face-to-face with my earliest fear: WATER. On this island, I was enveloped by the very thing I feared, teaching me daily lessons in trust. There, I was not only confronting my apprehensions but also finding myself falling more deeply in love with Him, as I was and continue to be continuously captivated by the magnificence of His creation.

He has carried me to that place I was Searching for. The place where I can honor Him with my emotions. The place where

I can learn to suffer with Him, learning to endure with Him by my side. The place where I can feel my feelings without being overwhelmed by them. The place where I learned not to lean solely on emotions but to embrace the One who controls all winds and waves. The place where I can rejoice in my sufferings, knowing that suffering produces endurance, endurance produces character, and character produces hope. The place where I can be still and know that He is God. The place where He does not demand that I suppress or deny my feelings. The place where He allows me to process them as He sits beside me, right here amid it all, In my tears, confusion, frustration, anger, disappointment, and questioning. In this place, I know His name, His nature as the God of my emotions, The One who fashioned me with care.

God's silence is painful, but I can be still and know because I know Him. I do not have to concern myself about the details. I can accost discomforts and things out of my control, given that I can look back over my life and see that God has revealed Himself to me time and time again. I do not have to fill myself with worries and concerns about tomorrow. Jesus offers a gentle reminder. "Consider the birds of the air and the lilies of the field" (Matthew 6:26-28). With this poetic imagery, He calls us to observe nature's simplicity and beauty. Birds do not sow or reap, yet they are always provided for. They wake each day without anxieties about their next meal or where they will find shelter. They sing they soar, and they live each moment fully, with the innate trust that the universe, in its grand design, will sustain them.

Then there are the lilies. They neither toil nor spin. They do not strive or labor, yet they are arrayed in splendor that even Solomon, in all his glory, could not match. These delicate flowers stand as a testament to the extravagance of God's care, painted in vibrant hues and swaying gracefully to the rhythm of creation. God is faithful when I am not. God is consistent when I am not. God loves me when I feel unworthy of His love. God is close even when I run away. God keeps His promises when I do not. God makes a way when there is no way. God speaks even when I ignore Him. God is good when I am not. God is perfect in all of His ways.

Through these examples, Jesus is not just supplying a lesson on His provision. He is also illustrating a way of life—a life of trust, contentment, and presence. It is an invitation to shed our anxieties and to embrace a life centered not on our own striving but on God's abundant grace. If God takes care of the birds that flutter by and the lilies that grow in the fields, how much more will He care for us, His children? With this assurance, we are encouraged to "seek first the kingdom of God and His righteousness," trusting that everything else we need will be added unto us.

I have grown to know God in multifaceted ways. He is a Father, a comfort in times of need, a steadfast shepherd, and a cherished friend. He mends wounds as a healer, paves the path as a way-maker, and soothes my thoughts as a mind regulator. He is the lover of my soul, my ever-present counselor, my resting place, and the compass steering me right. During chaos, He offers serenity; in uncertainty, He holds tomorrow. He is the wellspring of abundance, the sovereign King, and the ultimate savior. In moments of weakness, He fortifies me with strength, consistently proving His faithfulness as a promise keeper. Through His divine grace, He reignites and rejuvenates, making all things new. Yet, as I try to express my boundless gratitude through words, tears, and deeds, I realize they pale in comparison to His immeasurable love. Awe-struck and humbled, I find myself in the presence of a love so unexplainable that it transcends human comprehension. I can go back and say He did it right here, so I know I can trust Him in this.

In chapter one, we journeyed to the very dawn of creation, where the fundamental concepts of choice and consequence first took root. From the pages of Genesis to the revelations of the final testament, God's nature is clear. He remains consistent from the beginning to the end. As I reflect upon the chapters of my own life, I see the same narrative. Choices were made, seeds were sown, and even though times and circumstances shifted, one constant remained: the unchanging nature of God. Before moving to Hawaii, the recurring dream visited me once again. In this dream, I found myself on a beautiful island, the epitome of paradise. With a lantern as my guiding light, I'd walk through the inky night, its luminescence making me the lone beacon amidst the vast darkness. The massive, overpowering wave emerged unexpectedly, consuming both me and my source of light, leaving me gasping for breath in the shadowed waters.

On the eve of my trip, the narrative of this dream took an unexpected turn. As I walked, taking in the island's beauty, I saw the impending wave in the distance. A sense of dread consumed me, and the familiar words "Not again" escaped my lips. However, as I desperately searched for refuge, a mysterious man appeared before me. He halted my frantic escape, took the lantern from me, and set it securely at my feet. As our eyes met, a sense of understanding passed between us. Without uttering a word, his presence conveyed a silent reassurance.

The looming wave approached, but rather than engulfing me, it simply caressed my feet, leaving me untouched and astounded. This dream, I believe, was more than just a product of my subconscious. It was God's way of assuring me that even though life's storms are inevitable, His presence would be my guiding light. His word promised to illuminate my path, and this dream was a testament to that promise.

The waves of life might rise, attempting to drown, but they cannot submerge me, for He stands beside me, ensuring I remain unshaken. "The Lord is my shepherd; I shall not want. He maketh me to lie down in green pastures: he leadeth me beside the still waters. He restoreth my soul: he leadeth me in the paths of righteousness for his name's sake. Yea, though I walk through the valley of the shadow of death, I will fear no evil: for thou art with me; thy rod and thy staff they comfort me." - Psalm 23:1-4

The dream took me to Psalm 23. In the dream, the island and its beauty can be likened to the "green pastures" where God makes us lie down, a place of rest and rejuvenation. The impending wave in the dream is reminiscent of the "valley of the shadow of death," a place of uncertainty and fear. Yet, just as the mysterious man in the dream stood as my protector, ensuring the wave only caressed my feet, the psalmist speaks of God's rod and staff offering comfort in the face of danger. The "still waters" in the psalm can be seen as a reflection of the dream's initial setting.

Even though the waters rose tumultuously, in the end, they remained calm and gentle, symbolizing God's peace that surpasses all understanding. Both the dream and the psalm highlight that with God as our shepherd, we have nothing to fear. He is our protector, guide, and source of peace amidst life's storms.

When David writes of being led beside "still waters," he speaks to the calm and serenity that God brings into our lives, even during chaos. The still waters are a sanctuary, a place of reflection and peace. They represent the soothing presence of the Lord, where our souls find rest and our spirits are rejuvenated. Similarly, in my journey, God's command to "be still and know" echoes this same sentiment. In the moments of life's turmoil, uncertainties, and challenges, God didn't instruct me to panic, to run, or to fight. Instead, He beckoned me to find hope in His presence, to trust in His sovereignty, and to remain still in my faith.

My obedience to this command mirrors David's experience. By choosing to "be still," I allowed myself to be led by God to my own metaphorical "still waters." In this place of stillness, I not only found God's protective presence, as in the dream but also gained a deeper understanding and intimacy with Him. Just as still waters reflect the sky above, being still in God's presence allows us to reflect on His character, promises, and the depths of His love for us. The Lord is my shepherd, and I lack nothing!

The thing I feared most became my yearning. The water. Now, I am drawn to it. The rhythmic sound of waves lapping at the shore, the tang of its freshness in the air, the cool embrace of its depths, and the mysteries it holds. Each time I am near water, I sense the presence of my God meeting me right there in the middle of the ebb and flow. It is as if the waters bear testament to the times, and He displayed His power and sovereignty over each storm I faced.

I am reminded of the storm on the Sea of Galilee where Jesus, with a mere word, stilled the raging tempest (Matthew 8:23-27). I envision Peter stepping out in faith upon the waters, his eyes fixed on Jesus, defying nature's law. Then, there is Noah, faithfully navigating the deluge guided by a promise. Water, once a symbol of my fear, now echoes the stories of faith, trust, and God's presence. It has transformed into a canvas upon which I witness the artistry of God's power and love.

In the ever-evolving journey of my life, marked by mountaintop experiences and challenging valleys, I have come to know and experience God in His myriad dimensions deeply. Through every twist and turn, He has revealed Himself to me, guiding, nurturing, and anchoring me. Each name by which God is known in the scriptures paints the uniqueness of His character: Qanna "Jealous" (Exodus 20:5). He cherishes our relationship, desiring our full heart and devotion. This divine jealousy has shown up in my life not as a negative force but as a powerful reminder of God's deep love and desire for a close relationship with me. It is the gentle nudge when I have strayed from His path, urging me to return to His loving embrace. Qanna has been a driving force behind His pursuit of my heart, a fit of jealousy that seeks to protect and guide me toward a life filled with His blessings and purpose. It is a beautiful expression of His commitment to my spiritual well-being, a reminder that His love is steadfast and His desire for a thriving relationship with me is unmatched.

Jehovah Rapha, "The Lord That Heals" (Exodus 15:26). He has mended my heart and spirit time and again. Through the challenging experience of battling cancer, I witnessed God's healing power firsthand, which strengthened my belief in Him as a healer. "But He was pierced for our transgressions, He was crushed for our iniquities; the punishment that brought us peace was on Him, and by His wounds, we are healed" (Isaiah 53:5). This reminds me that God's love and grace are so deep that He bore our transgressions and iniquities, taking upon Himself the pain and suffering.

His sacrifice not only brought us peace but also served as a testament to His role as the ultimate healer. Time and time again, I have witnessed His healing touch in my life and in the lives of those around me. In moments of physical illness, emotional turmoil, or spiritual brokenness, I have turned to God in prayer, and His comforting presence has brought comfort and restoration. God's healing power extends beyond the physical, mending broken hearts and wounded spirits.

Jehovah Mekoddishkem, "The Lord Who Sanctifies You" or "Makes Holy" (Exodus 31:13). He purifies and sets me apart for His purposes. As a carpenter measures and cuts masterfully crafting each piece, so has God worked in my life, ensuring His design will not cease. He has mended broken parts of me with precision and loving care and reconstructed my shattered heart, restoring areas worn and bare. In moments I felt fragmented, He joined each piece to its place, carving out a destiny filled with purpose, love, and grace. Just as a carpenter shapes wood into something strong and new, God has been my Carpenter in everything I have been through. "Isn't this the carpenter? Isn't this Mary's son and the brother of James, Joseph, Judas, and Simon? Aren't his sisters here with us? And they took offense at him" (Mark 6: 3).

El Elyon, "The Most High God" (Genesis 14:18). In every situation I have faced, He has remained sovereign, the highest authority to whom I turn to. In life's desert, where drought often nears, where hope can diminish and give way to tears, I found a source so pure and so nigh. God has been my well that never runs dry. When I felt parched from the world's scorching heat, His promises flowed, making my journey complete. In moments of despair, when strength started to wane, I drank from His eternal well and was sustained.

He quenched my deepest thirst, renewed my spirit, and lifted me high. Through trials and storms, when I felt I might cry, His presence remained a wellspring nearby. To the world, I declare, God has been my well, that never runs dry." But whoever drinks the water I give them will never thirst. Indeed, the water I give them will become in them a spring of water welling up to eternal life" (John 4:14).

Jehovah Raah "The Lord Our Shepherd" (Psalms 23). He tenderly leads, nurtures, and protects me. In moments of abandonment, I found assurance in the fact that God is a Father to the fatherless and a mother to the motherless. "The Spirit you received does not make you slaves so that you live in fear again; rather, the Spirit you received brought about your adoption to sonship. And by him we cry, 'Abba, Father'" (Romans 8:15). Through faith, I have been adopted by God, and He has become both a loving mother and father to me. As I embraced His presence, I discovered a deep sense of belonging and acceptance akin to a child finding comfort in a parent's embrace.

God, through His Holy Spirit, had nurtured and guided me, offering maternal care in times of tenderness and paternal strength when I needed it most. In moments of fear or uncertainty, I have found comfort in crying out, "Abba, Father," knowing that His love knows no bounds and He encompasses the roles of both parent figures in my life. This divine adoption has filled my heart with a sense of love, security, and purpose, enriching my relationship with God in ways beyond measure.

El Shaddai The "Lord God Almighty," the "All-Sufficient One" (Genesis 17:1). He has been my rock, supplying abundantly even when I thought all was lost. In the heartbreaking process of a divorce, when I felt broken, God was my sustainer, a potter. He held me together. "Yet you, LORD, are our Father. We are the clay; you are the potter; we are all the work of your hand" (Isaiah 64:8). I have come to recognize the masterful hands of God, shaping me much like a potter molds clay. Each experience, whether joyful or painful, has been a deliberate touch, a gentle press, or sometimes a firm reshape. Even in moments when I felt misshapen or cracked, it was His hands that centered me on the wheel, spinning and sculpting me toward His divine design. Every ridge, every curve in the vessel of my being bears the mark of His intentionality. There were times I felt pressure, unsure of His plan, but in retrospect, I see a form, a purpose, a masterpiece crafted by the Greatest Potter. My essence, my purpose, and my journey are a testament to His ceaseless workmanship. Truly, in knowing Him as my Potter, I have come to understand my value and purpose as His cherished creation.

Jehovah Jireh "The Lord Will Provide" (Genesis 22:14). In moments of lack and need, He has always made a way. God has been the Bread of Life. In the diverse banquet of life where various experiences offer tastes of joy, sorrow, triumph, and trial, I have come to realize the truth: God is my sustenance, the bread of life that fuels my soul. Just as bread nourishes the body, He revitalizes my spirit, ensuring I am never left wanting. In moments of emptiness or spiritual hunger, it is His words and presence that fill me, supplying both comfort and strength.

No worldly feast or temporary delight can compare to the fulfillment He brings. When I partake in His teachings and commune with Him in prayer, I am assured of an eternal satisfaction that neither fades nor falters. By knowing Him as the bread of life, I have discovered an enduring nourishment, a sustenance that transcends the ephemeral and feeds the eternal within me. "Then Jesus declared, 'I am the bread of life. Whoever comes to me will never go hungry, and whoever believes in me will never be thirsty'" (John 6:35).

Jehovah Sabaoth, "The Lord of Hosts" or "Powers" (1 Samuel 1:3). He commands the heavens and Earth, ensuring I am never alone. During restless nights, when my mind couldn't find rest, I found peace in Him. He is my resting place. "Come to me, all you who are weary and burdened, and I will give you rest" (Matthew 11:28). In the ceaseless whirlwind of life, with its unending demands, challenges, and noise, I have found an oasis of serenity in God. Amidst the clamor and chaos, He beckons me with a gentle invitation, offering consolation to my weary soul.

When the weight of the world threatens to press down upon me, it is in His embrace that I find relief, a shelter where burdens are lifted and anxieties dissipate. To know Him is to know a haven of peace, a resting place where I am not just restored but rejuvenated. Even when storms rage around me, in His presence, I find a stillness, a grounding force that assures me of safety and love. Truly, in recognizing Him as my resting place, I have unearthed the depth of tranquility and rest that only He can provide.

Elohim, "God," "Judge," "Creator" (Genesis 1:1). He is the origin of all things and has crafted my journey with a divine plan. Master, "You call me 'Teacher' and 'Lord,' and rightly so, for that is what I am" (John 13:13). In the classroom of existence where life unfolds its myriad lessons, I have discerned a singular, guiding force: God, my Master. His teachings, both gentle and challenging, have steered my path, directing me toward righteousness and wisdom. As a pupil looks to their teacher for instruction and understanding, so do I turn to Him for direction and discernment. To acknowledge Him as my Master is to willingly place myself under His guidance, trusting in His plans and purposes for my life.

In doing so, I have found clarity amidst confusion and purpose amidst perplexity. His authority is not one of dominance but of divine love, always seeking my highest good. By truly recognizing Him as my Master, I have embraced a journey of growth, learning, and unending grace.

Jehovah Nissi "The Lord My Banner" (Exodus 17:15). In battles, both external and internal, He has been my rallying point. In the vast narrative of humanity, punctuated by moments of despair, loss, and sin, emerges a beacon of hope, a Savior, Christ the Lord. The birth of this Savior in the humble city of David was not merely a historical event but a personal revelation to me. Through every misstep, every faltering moment of doubt, it has been His redemptive love that has lifted me up. I have come to understand salvation not just as a distant theological concept but as an intimate, transformative experience.

Christ, as my Savior, has freed me from chains I didn't even realize they bound me, granting me a renewed spirit and purpose. The weight of my transgressions and the shadow of my regrets are dispelled by the radiant light of His saving grace. To know Him is to know liberation, forgiveness, and an unfathomable love that seeks to save even the lost. "For unto you is born this day in the city of David a Savior, who is Christ the Lord." (Luke 2:11).

Yahweh, The "Lord Jehovah," "ever-present and ever faithful" (Genesis 2:4). In a world where promises are often made lightly and broken effortlessly, I have found constancy in God, the ultimate Promise Keeper. Each commitment He has made, every word He has spoken, resonates with truth and faithfulness. When I have felt adrift in seas of uncertainty or walked through valleys of doubt, it has been His promises that have anchored my soul and lit my path. The scripture affirms that all His promises find their affirmation in Him, an echoing "Yes" and a resounding "Amen." Through every season of life, in moments of elation and epochs of despair, He has never faltered in His commitment to me. To know Him is to know the epitome of reliability, a steadfastness that not only keeps promises but glorifies them, revealing His immutable love and grace. "For all the promises of God in Him are Yes, and in Him Amen, to the glory of God through us" (2 Corinthians 1:20).

Jehovah Tsidkenu "The Lord Is Righteousness" (Jeremiah 23:6). He has been my moral compass, guiding me towards what is right. Where paths often twist in unexpected ways, and darkness sometimes seems to obscure the way forward, I have found guidance in God's Word, the lamp upon my feet. It has been the radiant beacon that has illuminated my steps, ensuring I do not stumble or lose my way. In moments of confusion, when I've stood at life's crossroads, uncertain of which way to turn, the scriptures have shed light, revealing the direction divinely ordained for me.

This lamp has not merely been a distant, external guide; it has penetrated the depths of my soul, enlightening my innermost thoughts and desires. By relying on His Word, I have navigated challenges with clarity and faced uncertainties with confidence. To know His Word is to know a light that never falters, a lamp that forever brightens my path. "Your word is a lamp for my feet, a light on my path" (Psalm 119:105). Righteousness comes from God alone, and through faith and obedience to Him, we can be made righteous.

Adoni, "Lord" and "Master" (Genesis 15:2). He has been my guiding force, leading my steps with purpose. When everything around me was chaotic, God was the firm foundation that kept me grounded. "For no one can lay any foundation other than the one already laid, which is Jesus Christ" (1 Corinthians 3:11). I have come to know God as my firm foundation, the unshakable cornerstone upon which I build my beliefs and values. Through moments of introspection and faith, I have found succor in His presence, knowing that even in the stormiest of times, His unconditional love and guidance provide stability and purpose. It is through prayer, meditation, and the study of sacred texts that I have forged a deep connection with God, solidifying His role as the bedrock of my existence. This relationship not only grants me strength and resilience but also fills my heart with gratitude and a sense of purpose.

Jehovah Shalom "The Lord Is Peace" (Judges 6:24). In tumultuous times, He has been my calm. When I felt lost in my own thoughts and unstable in my mind, God provided me with the strength to stand firm, and I came to know Him as a mind regulator. "And the peace of God, which transcends all understanding, will guard your hearts and your minds in Christ Jesus" (Philippians 4:7).

I have experienced the truth in this scripture. In moments of doubt, anxiety, or confusion, I turn to God in prayer and find a deep, indescribable peace that settles my troubled mind. It is a peace that defies logic and surpasses my comprehension, reminding me of His loving presence and reassuring me that He guards and guides my thoughts and emotions. Through this intimate connection with God, I have discovered the transformative power of faith in regulating my mind, bringing serenity, clarity, and purpose even in life's most challenging moments, even when things do not make sense.

Jehovah Shammah "The Lord Is There" (Ezekiel 48:35). In moments of loneliness and desolation, I have found safety knowing He is with me. When fear threatened to take hold of my heart, He was my safety. "The name of the LORD is a fortified tower; the righteous run to it and are safe" (Proverbs 18:10). It is in moments of seeking God that I have felt His protective embrace, a shield against life's storms. Whether facing personal challenges, fears, or trials, I have found reassurance in knowing that God is my ultimate safety net. The more I seek God In the vastness of oceans deep. I find Him Where mysteries and wonders sleep, and I know the depth of His love for me. Amidst waves that crash and span, there, I find Him, where my faith stands.

El Olam Denoting the "Everlasting God," "God of Eternity," "God of the Universe," and "God of Ancient Days"

(Genesis 21:33). His timeless nature assures me that He oversees all seasons of my life. Just as He has carried me through the pages of this book, I know that His voice will remain my compass, pointing the way to hope, peace, and a deeper connection with Him. In the stillness of my heart, that still small voice, I hear His sacred echoes, reminding me that I am never alone and that His presence will always carry me through whatever lies ahead.

Dawna Lindsey

Lord,

I thank you for this time of communion. I am thankful that you know exactly what I need and that you are the supplier of every need I have. I needed this time and space to grieve and be comforted, fall apart and be made whole, be weak and made strong, this space to exhale and let my tears flow. You have carried me to the place where I can be still and know that you are God. The places where I can honor You with every emotion I feel, casting all of my cares on You. The place where I can allow The Creator space to create. The place where I allow The Savior to save me. The place of deliverance where I am set free from everything that has weighed me down. This place of peace. I was like a sheep, lost in the wilderness of sin, wandering aimlessly and afraid. But You are a shepherd, seeking me out with gentle care and agape love. You left the ninety-nine to find the one and carry me on Your shoulders back to safety (Luke 15:4-7). I was like a clay pot, fragile and flawed, prone to breaking and cracking. But You are like a potter, shaping and molding me with Your skilled hands. You can take the clay that has marred and make it new again, filling it with Your grace and glory (Isaiah 64:8). I was like a tree, rooted in the soil of my past, growing tall and strong but bearing the scars of the storms I have weathered. But You are

143

like a gardener, nurturing me with Your living water and pruning me with Your wise hands. You can help me grow in Your likeness, bearing fruit that will last (John 15:1-5). I was like a prodigal child, wandering far from Your loving embrace, wasting my inheritance on empty pleasures and vain pursuits. But You are a good Father, waiting and watching for me to return, running towards me with open arms, embracing me with tears of joy. You can restore me to Your family and throw a feast of celebration in my honor (Luke 15:11-32). I am Yours, and You are mine. Your love for me is deeper than the ocean, wider than the sky, higher than the mountains, and longer than the ages. You have called me by name, and I am Yours forever (Isaiah 43:1). As I listen to the tranquil flow of water, I realize how I have been caught up in things not meant for me. For nothing this world could offer can compare to the euphoria of being with You. Thank You for your forgiveness. Thank You for grace. Thank You for peace. Thank you that everything that has something to do with me concerns You. Thank You for being God.

Dawna Lindsey